The Menu Dictionary

Words and Ways of the
International Restaurant World

Bon Appétit!

Vicki Luckett

For The
  – Diner
    – Server
      – Reader of food literature

The Menu Dictionary
Words and Ways of the International Restaurant World
by Victoria Luckett
with Leah La Plante

Don't dine out without it!

The destiny of nations depends upon what and how they eat.
– Jean-anthelme Brillat-Savarin

The Menu Dictionary
Words and Ways of the International Restaurant World

by Victoria Luckett
with Leah La Plante

Copyright © 1999 by Victoria Luckett and Leah La Plante

Published by   Sweetwater Press
                   7798 S.W. 99th Street
                   Miami, Florida 33156
                   Telephone/Fax: 305-271-9781
                   SweetwaterPress@earthlink.net

Acknowledgements:
                   Printer: Fine Printing, Miami, Florida
                   Cover Design: Maurice Millan

Cartoons: The New Yorker Collection - from Cartoonbank.com
                   All rights reserved.
                   Charles Saxon - 1972, page 45.
                   Chon Day - 1977, page v.
                   Charles Sauers - 1984, page 127.
                   Henry Martin - 1988, page 102.
                   J.B. Handelsman - 1993, page 129.
                   P C Vey - 1999, page 91, 108.

Library of Congress Cataloging-in-Publication Data:
Card Catalog Number: 99-95098
Luckett, Victoria and Leah La Plante
The Menu Dictionary: Words and Ways of the International Restaurant World /
Victoria Luckett, Leah La Plante. - 1st Edition.
ISBN 0-9673014-0-8 (pbk.)
1. Restaurant menu dictionary and guide.

Printed in the United States of America.
1 0 9 8 7 6 5 4 3 2 1

Je vis de bonne soupe et non de beau langage.
It is good food and not fine words that keeps me alive.
– Molière

Table of Contents

One cannot think well, love well,
sleep well if one has not dined well.
        – Virginia Woolf

The Menu Dictionary

The art of dining well is no slight art.
— Michel de Montaigne

Preface

The word "restaurant" was coined in France (of course!) in 1765 with food purveyor Boulanger's sign (in Latin): *Venite ad me omnes que stomacho laboratis et ego restaurabo vos.* – Come to me all you whose stomachs suffer and I will retore you. The sign later said it all with just the word *restaurabo* (to restore) – our word restaurant.

Indeed, when we are seated in a dining establishment and pick up the menu (also from the French: *Menu de repas* - list of items for a meal, shortened by 1837 to menu), we think of sustenance, yes, but we desire much more than simply to soothe our suffering stomachs. Andre Simon wisely makes the plea that "The first of all considerations is that our meals shall be fun as well as fuel." As the *Bible* says: "A man hath no better thing under the sun than to eat, and to drink, and to be merry" (Ecclesiastes 8:15).

Such a three-part at-table experience hopefully does restore us, but . . . unfortunately, not always. We delight in being spontaneous, and taking risks: a new or unfamiliar cafe or brasserie, no reservations, ordering a dish described in "chefese", that mysterious language one frequently runs into on menus.
The Menu Dictionary to the rescue!

Much has happened in the food world since Julia Child's "The French Chef" television series, launched in 1963, popularized fine food. In 1977, The American Culinary Federation persuaded The U.S. Department of Labor to reclassify chefs as professionals rather than domestics. Today, chefs are major cultural figures. Restaurant dining is an extremely popular form of entertainment. "huge numbers of baby-boomers now have sophisticated tastes," says Cheryl Russell, editor of *The Boomer Report.*

"For God's sake, stop picking at it!"

Consider that today Americans on average eat out at restaurants 4.1 times a week (up from 3.8 in 1994). 45 percent of every food dollar is spent on eating out, always with the hope of satisfying the head and heart as well as the stomach. Mark Twain said that "to eat is human, to digest is divine," but you don't digest divinely as a frustrated hostess or host if you and your companions (literally to eat bread - *panis* - with one's comrades), are not pleased with the food preparation or wine choices.

The Menu Dictionary to the rescue! In this convenient, takealong-size book is a diner-supportive, simplified arrangement of carefully researched, up-to-date features that are designed to give today's worldly-wise restaurant patrons (as well as the service personnel, who must keep up with their questions), the know-how needed to feel comfortable and satisfied during all the stages of becoming well-nourished, merry all the while! – no slight art!

The Features:

1. An A to Z of the more common lesser-known food and beverage words (with pronunciation as needed) from menus of all cuisine nationalities.

2. Blank pages at the end, for you to add menu words.

3. The other-than-menu language and the know-how involved in truly satisfying restaurant dining.

   The words: grazing, menu degustation, tapas, majordomo, New World Cuisine – and many more!

   The ways: making reservations, special requests, tipping, handling the bill, health issues, and much more!

4. Tip table – inside back cover.

5. Bibliography: a select list of books, magazines, general and internet information for the beginner-to-the-advanced food lover.

Final thoughts:

> *In a restaurant, choose a table near a waiter.*
> *– Jewish proverb*

> *Epitaph for a waiter: God finally caught his eye.*
> *– George S. Kaufman*

> *Eat, drink, and be merry, for tomorrow we diet!*
> *– Anonymous*

> *Ask not what you can do for your country – ask what's for lunch.*
> *– Orson Welles*

> *When going to an eating house, go to one that is full of customers.* *– Chinese proverb*

> *Everything you see I owe to spaghetti.* *– Sophia Loren*

> *I say it's spinach, and I say to hell with it!* *– E.B. White*

> *Wine is sure proof that God loves us and wants us to be happy.*
> *– Benjamin Franklin*

> *I drink to the general joy of the whole table!*
> *– William Shakespeare*

$\mathcal{T}$he Menu Dictionary

Poached eggs on ghost.
  – James Joyce

Every fruit has its secret.
  – D.H. Lawrence

When asked at dinner which dish he (Thoreau) preferred,
he replied, "The nearest".
  – Emerson

Satisfy your hearts with food and wine
for herein is courage and strength.
  – Homer

Introduction

"Waiter, is there a translator in the house for the menu?" That's the question *New York Times* food critic Alex Witchel asks in a recent article. In the 80s, menus were about whimsy (familiarity) – in the 90s, culinary obscurity. Today's clientele is better-educated, world-traveled, TV-internet-broadened. Restaurants are responding in one way by reaching out to – the cutting edge. That's cool, but what <u>AM</u> I sinking my trembling fork into when I order "blue corn quesadilla with roasted poblano rojas, pepper jack, and cilantro sour crema?"

One can ask the waiter, of course, but with the daunting complexity of today's menus, the growing number of restaurants and the turnover of service personnel, there is also a challenge for those on the other side of the table. Besides, some diners-out don't want to get into an intellectual conversation about their order, but rather prefer to with relative ease select something tasty-sounding, whether an old familiar dish or the latest experimental gustation, and sit back with a soothing drink.

The Menu Dictionary to the rescue! The dictionary's takealong size, its simple A to Z listing, is designed to be a useful as well as a pleasure-enhancing aid for both diner and server – Don't dine out without it!

The words are from menus of all cuisine nationalities. Pronunciation is indicated when necessary. For example: Ajillo – Spanish, *aHEyo*, (accent on the capitalized letters), garlic sauce. Words in the definitions that are in **bold** print are listed in the dictionary.

There are blank pages at the end for additional menu words.

If restaurants had windows into their souls,
they would likely be in the form of menus.
– Diane Kochilas, Psychologist

In a restaurant I order everything I don't want, so I have a lot
to play around with while everybody else is eating.
– Andy Warhol

À la mode: A dessert served with ice cream as a topping.

Acidulate: To make slightly acid.

Ackee and saltfish [Jamaica]**:** Sauteed ackee (a reddish-orange fruit) and salt cod, flavored with chilies, garlic, onion and spices.

Adobo: A thick *soy* and vinegar sauce used for squid.

Age gyoza [Japanese]**:** Deep fried pork dumpling appetizer.

Agnolotti [Italian]**:** Small half-moon-shaped pasta stuffed with meat and/or cheese.

Aguacate [Spanish]**:** Avocado, a tropical fruit eaten raw, in salads and in *guacamole*.

Aioli *(aOle)*: Garlic-flavored mayonnaise.

Ajillo [Spanish] *(aHEyo)*: Garlic sauce.

Albacore tuna: Light flesh, mild-flavored high (good) fat *tuna*.

Alcapurias [West Indies]**:** A side dish of mashed green bananas or yuca (a potato-like tuber also known as cassava and manioc) filled with seasoned ground beef and vegetables, formed into flattened ovals and deep-fried.

Almondine

Almondine: Served or prepared with almonds.

Almuerzo [Spanish]: Lunch.

Aloo bainghan [Indian-India]: Eggplant and potato cooked with spices, especially *cilantro*.

Amaretto: An Italian liqueur with a slightly bitter almond flavor.

Ancho: A chili pepper, ranging in flavor from mild to pungent. In its fresh, green state it is referred to as a poblano chili.

Anchovy: A small, salty fish used especially for sauces and relishes. Often served with caesar salad.

Andouille sausage: Spicy, heavily smoked sausage made from pork and/or beef intestines and spices. A specialty of *Cajun* cooking.

Angel hair [Italian] capelli d'angelo: The thinnest form of pasta.

Angelina [Italian]: Pasta sauce made with fresh tomatoes, *arugula*, sundried tomatoes, garlic and olive oil.

Angler fish: Also known as monk fish and by other names. Low-fat and firm-textured, with a mild, sweet, lobster-like flavor.

Angnolotti [Italian]: Pasta filled with cheese in a light cream sauce.

Anis (Anise): Licorice.

Antipasto [Italian]: "Before the pasta". Hot or cold **hors d'oeuvres**, such as cheese, smoked meats, olives, and **marinated** vegetables.

Antojitos [Nicaragua] *(antoHEtos)*: Snacks.

Apéritif [French] *(ahpairuhTEEF)*: A light alcoholic drink taken before a meal to stimulate the appetite, such as champagne and sherry.

Apetitosa [Italian]: Pasta sauce made with mild Italian sausage and mushrooms in a spicy marinara sauce.

Apfelpfannkuchen [German]: A dessert. A large pancake filled with thinly sliced spiced apples, served with a variety of sweet toppings.

Arancio [Italian] *(arANseo)*: An orange, basil and sherry wine sauce for veal.

Arborio rice [Italian] *(arBOReo)*: A short, fat, high-starch rice that when cooked has a creamy texture.

Arni psito me patates [Greek]: Marinated lamb roasted with potatoes.

Arni tis souvias [Greek]: Marinated and barbecued leg of lamb.

Arroz amarillo [Spanish] *(ahROSE amarEyo)*: Yellow rice.

Arroz blanco

Arroz blanco: White rice.

Arroz con pollo [Spanish] *(ahROSE con POYo)*: Chicken and rice.

Arugula: Mediterranean salad green (rocket, roquette).

Asiago cheese [Italian] *(ahseAHgo)*: A semi-firm cheese with a rich, nutty flavor.

Asopao [Puerto Rican]: A soupy chicken, meat or seafood stew with rice and a variety of vegetables and flavorings, depending upon the cook.

Atun [Spanish]: *Tuna* fish.

Au gratin [French] *(og GRAHtin)*: A dish cooked or baked with a topping of either browned bread crumbs and butter or grated cheese, or both.

Au jus [French] *(oZHOO)*: Served in the natural juices that flow from the meat as it is cooked.

Au poivre [French] *(oPWAHV)*: Spiced with peppercorns or ground black pepper.

Auberge [French]: In France, a country inn with lodging. In the U.S., a restaurant with a country atmosphere.

Avgolemono [Greek]: Both a soup and a sauce, made of chicken broth, egg yolks and lemon juice. Rice is added to the soup.

Avocado (Alligator pear): A large, pear-shaped tropical fruit eaten raw, usually in salads.

Baba ghanoush [Mediterranean] *(BAba guhNOOSH)*: A puree of charred eggplant, *tahini*, olive oil, lemon juice and salt.

Bacalao: Codfish.

Baklava [Turkish]: A dessert of chopped nuts sandwiched between thin layers of *filo* pastry and coated in syrup.

Balzamic vinegar: Vinegar made from white trebbiano grape juice, getting its dark color and pungent sweetness from special aging in wooden barrels.

Banger [British]: Slang for a number of types of sausages made of ground pork or beef with bread crumbs and spices.

Basil: An aromatic herb of the mint family with purplish-green oval leaves, a basic ingredient of *pesto* sauce.

Basmanti rice: Narrow and long-shaped rice from India, with a pungent fragrance and faintly nutty flavor.

Batido: A milk shake made with tropical fruit (guanabana, mamey, fruta bomba, etc.)

Béarnaise sauce [French] *(berNAZE)*: A sauce made with egg yolks, **shallots**, **tarragon**, butter, vinegar and sometimes white wine and chopped **chervil**.

Beijing [Chinese] *(bayZHING)*: The site of the imperial court and therefore the most sophisticated of the regional Chinese cuisines, lightly seasoned, with much use of garlic.

Bella luna [Italian]: Pasta sauce made with cream, **porcini** mushrooms and sundried tomatoes.

Beurre blanc [French] *(burBLAHN)*: A **reduction** sauce of wine vinegar and **shallots** cooked with butter and beaten until thick and foamy.

Beurre noir [French] *(bur NWAR)*: A **reduction** sauce of darkly browned butter flavored with herbs and vinegar.

Beurre noisette [French] *(burnwasET)*: A **reduction** sauce of butter cooked until golden or nut brown, flavored with **capers**, vinegar, herbs, etc.

Biscotti [Italian]: A variously-flavored twice-baked cookie that is made by first being baked in a loaf, then slicing the loaf and baking the slices, making an extremely crunchy cookie that is perfect for dipping into coffee or dessert wine.

Bisque *(bisk)*: A thick, cream soup, especially of *pureed* shellfish.

Bisque de homard [French]: Soup made with *pureed* and diced lobster meat, white wine, *cognac* and fresh cream.

Bistec de lomo [Spanish]: *Delmonico* steak.

Bistec de rinonada [Spanish] *(BIStec de rinyonAHda)*: New York strip steak.

Black Forest cake: A cake based on chocolate sponge and decorated with whipped cream, cherries and chocolate curlicues.

Blackened: Coated with spices and *sautéed* quickly over high heat so that the outside chars.

Blaff [French-speaking West Indian]: Fish, such as red *snapper*, *marinated* and *poached* with such ingredients as chilies, garlic, lime and seasonings.

Blanched: Quickly boiled (vegetables or fruit), then plunged into ice water, to tenderize, remove skin, or intensify color.

Bleu cheese: A rich cheese in which the internal mold manifests itself in blue veins. Made in France esp. with sheep's milk, and elsewhere from cow's and goat's milk.

Blintze *(BLINce)*: A *crepe* filled with cream cheese and cottage cheese and grilled or fried.

Bo nhung dam [Vietnamese]: Beef cooked at the table in a seasoned broth, served with a variety of accompaniments, such as rice paper, mint and pickled vegetables.

Bo xao xa ot [Vietnamese]: Sliced beef *sautéed* with lemongrass, peanuts and chilies.

Bocconcino [Italian] *(boconSEno)*: A sauce for chicken prepared with asparagus, *porcini* mushrooms and *fontina* cheese.

Boeuf bordelaise [French]: Beef, usually broiled, in a sauce made with red or white wine, brown stock, bone *marrow*, *shallots*, parsley and herbs.

Boeuf bourguignonne [French]: Beef *braised* in red wine, *garnished* with small mushrooms and white onions.

Bok choy [Chinese]: Chinese cabbage.

Bollito misto [Italian]: A classic Italian dish – mixed boiled meats with a highly-flavored sauce.

Bologuese [Italian]: Pasta sauce made with a thick blend of *marinated* tomato sauce, ground beef, green peppers, garlic and onion.

Bombay aloo [Indian-India]: Potatoes *sautéed* with a selection of spices and mustard seed.

Bombe *(bahm)*: A molded frozen dessert consisting of layers of ice cream or sherbet, usually served with a dessert sauce.

Bordelaise [French] *(bordeLAZE)*: A brown sauce flavored with red wine and **shallots** and **garnished** with **poached marrow** and parsley.

Borscht [Russian]: Beetroot soup, with beef broth and other vegetables, especially cabbage.

Boudin blanc [French]: Translates as "white pudding," but is the name of delicate sausage made with pork, chicken, fat, eggs, cream, breadcrumbs and seasonings, usually gently **sautéed** and served hot.

Bouillabaisse [French] *(BOOLyaBAZE)*: A soup or stew containing several types of fish and often shellfish, usually combined with olive oil, tomatoes and **saffron**.

Bouquet garni *(boocay garNA)*: A selection of herbs tied in a bundle and added for flavoring to soup, stews, etc. while they are cooking, and later removed.

Bourguignonne [French] *(boorgeeNYON)*: Meat (usually beef) **braised** in red wine, garnished with small mushrooms and white onions.

Boursin cheese *(boorSAHN)*: A white and smooth cheese with a buttery texture, often flavored with herbs, garlic or cracked pepper.

Braised: Meat, fish or vegetables cooked by **sautéeing** in oil and then **simmering** in a small amount of liquid.

Brandade

Brandade [Spanish]: A pounded mixture of salted or smoked fish, olive oil, garlic, milk and cream.

Brandy: A liquor distilled from wine or other fermented grape juice and aged in wood, which contributes flavor and color.

Bratwurst [German]: A type of pork sausage.

Brazier: A pan for holding hot coals; a utensil in which food is exposed to heat through a wire grill.

Bread and butter pudding [Irish]: A light combination of layered toasted bread, raisins and almonds baked in a custard.

Breadfruit: A large tropical vegetable similar in texture and flavor to squash.

Bresaola [Italian]: Thin slices of cured beef.

Brie *(bre)*: A soft white cow's milk cheese.

Brioche *(breOSH)*: A soft roll or small loaf made from a rich yeast-raised dough of flour, butter and eggs.

Brochette [French] *(broSHET)*: A skewer (long pin of wood or metal) used in cooking.

Brunoise [French] *(brunWAHZ)*: A mixture of vegetables that have been finely diced or shredded, then cooked slowly in butter. Used to flavor soups and sauces.

Brunswick stew: [Brunswick County, Virginia – 1828.] A hearty meat (traditionally squirrel) and onion stew with a variety of vegetables, such as lima beans, okra and corn.

Bruschetta: Garlic bread.

Buffalo mozzarella: In southern Italy, where it originated, mozzarella cheese is made from buffalo's milk.

Buñuelo [Spanish] *(bunyouELo)*: Deep fried special dough, sprinkled with sugar and cinnamon syrup and served with vanilla ice cream.

Burdock: Slender root vegetable with a rusty brown skin and grayish-white flesh. Also called gobo.

Burgoo [The U.S. South]: Also called Kentucky burgoo – a thick stew of meat (originally squirrel or rabbit) and vegetables.

Burgundy: A red (sometimes white) wine that is robust and full-bodied.

Burrito [Mexican] *(burEtoe)*: A flour ***tortilla*** folded and rolled to completely enclose any of several savory fillings, including shredded or chopped meat, refried beans, grated cheese.

Cabernet Sauvignon *(caberNA sovinYON)*: A dry, red wine, usually from the Bordeaux region of France and northern California.

Cacciatore [Italian] *(catchuhTORe)*: A red sauce for chicken containing tomatoes, onions, bell peppers, and spices.

Caesar salad: A salad of romaine lettuce tossed with an olive oil dressing, garlic and grated cheese, topped with croutons and sometimes ***anchovies***.

Cafe con leche [Spanish] *(cafa con LAche)*: Coffee with milk.

Caffe latte: Espresso with steamed milk.

Caffe mocha ghirandelli *(cafa Mokuh giranDELe)*: Espresso coffee, chocolate, and milk.

Cajun: A style of cooking that combines French and Southern cuisines.

Cajun popcorn [Louisianan]: Shelled, batter-coated, deep-fried crawfish tails – a popular snack served with a spicy tomato sauce.

Calamari [Italian]: Squid.

Calamari ripieni [Italian]: Squid stuffed with herbs and **anchovy** paste, **sautéed** with onion, wine, tomatoes and herbs.

Caldo gallego [Spanish] *(CALdo gaiAgo)*: White bean soup.

California (Sushi) roll [Japanese]: Rice roll with cucumber, **avocado** and crab.

Callaloo [Caribbean]: Soup made with callaloo greens, okra, and meat, such as seafood or pork, and a variety of seasonings.

Calmar a l'escabeche [French]
(calMAR ah LEScoBACHe):
Hors d'oeuvre: Calamari (squid) cooked in olive oil, onions, herbs and garlic.

Calvados [French]: A dry apple **brandy**, often used in cooking.

Calzone [Italian] (calZOne): A stuffed pizza. The filling can be various meats, vegetables, and usually **mozzarella** cheese. Calzones may be deep-fried or brushed with olive oil and baked.

Camarones [Spanish]: Shrimp.

Canard [French]: Duck.

Canh chua ca [Vietnamese]: Hot-and-sour soup.

Cannelloni [Italian]: Pasta in the form of little tubes.

Cantonese [Chinese]: The most Americanized and simply flavored Chinese cuisine – less hot and spicy, with an emphasis on sauces (especially chicken broth), stirfrying, and steaming.

Capellini [Italian]: Angel hair, the thinnest form of strand pasta.

Caper: The berry of an herbaceous plant, usually bottled in a mild pickling liquid.

Capesanate [Italian] *(cahpeSAHNte)*: Scallop.

Cappuccino: Espresso coffee and steamed milk, often served with powdered cinnamon and topped with foam made from steamed milk.

Carambola *(cahramBOluh)*: A greenish yellow subtropical/tropical fruit that is served in star-shaped slices.

Caramelized: Converted to or covered with caramel (cooked sugar).

Carbonade [French]: A thick stew of beef, onions, herbs, etc., cooked in beer.

Cardamom: A member of the ginger family, the seeds of which have a pungent aroma and a warm, spicy-sweet flavor.

Carne [Spanish] *(CARne)*: Meat.

Carne asada al jugo [Spanish] *(CARne ahSAHduh ahl Ugo)*: Roast beef Cuban style.

Carne de Congrejo Sazonado [Spanish]: Seasoned crabmeat.

Carozza [Italian] *(carOzuh)*: Red pepper cream sauce with a touch of **anchovy**.

Carp: A fish that is often found in muddy waters, which can give a mossy flavor to the lean, white flesh.

Carpaccio [Italian} *(carPAHchio)*: An appetizer of thinly sliced raw beef, often served with shavings of **parmesan** cheese and a **vinaigrette** or other piquant sauce.

Cascos de guayaba con queso crema [Spanish]: **Guava** shells with cream cheese.

Cassava (yuca) [Spanish]: Any of several tropical plants, cultivated for their starchy, tuberous roots, used as a potato, and as the source of tapioca.

Cassolette *(casoLA)*: A container for cooking and serving an individual portion of food, usually made of pottery, silver, or paper, or sometimes of baked dough.

Cassoulet [French] *(casoLA)*: A rich stew of **haricot** beans and assorted meats.

Catharina [Italian]: Pasta sauce with cream, **pancetta**, green peas, **parmesan** cheese and mushrooms.

Cayenne: A hot, biting **condiment**.

Cellophane noodles (Foon shee) [Chinese]:
Bean threads, made from mung bean flour.

Cena [Spanish] *(SAYnuh)*: Dinner.

Cernia [Italian]: Grouper.

Ceviche *(suhVEche)*: An appetizer of small pieces of
raw fish **marinated** in lime or lemon juice, served
with onions, peppers, and spices.

Caille farcie en croute Lucullus [French]:
Quail stuffed with goose liver and **truffles**.

Cha gio [Vietnamese]: Pork or seafood, cellophane
noodles and vegetables wrapped in rice paper and
deep-fried.

Chablis *(shaBLE)*: White wine with a crisp, dry flavor,
and a decided metallic quality.

Champignon [French] *(shampeNYOHN)*: Mushroom.

Chanterelle: A bright yellow to orange mushroom
with a delicate, nutty, sometimes fruity flavor and a
somewhat chewy texture.

Chantilly: Sweetened whipped cream.

Chao tom [Vietnamese]: Shrimp paste grilled on
sugarcane.

Char sue din [Chinese]: Diced roast pork.

Charcuterie [French]: A store in which pork products
– ham, sausage, **pâté**, etc., are sold.

Chard: A beet whose large leaves and succulent stalks are often cooked as a vegetable.

Chardonnay: A white wine, generally rich, buttery, fruity, and on the dry side.

Chasseur [French]: A sauce of mushrooms, *shallots* or onions, tomatoes, and white wine.

Chateaubriand [French] *(shatobreAHND)*: A thick slice of *tenderloin*, broiled and served with potatoes and a sauce, often a *bearnaise* sauce.

Chervil: A mild, slightly anise-flavored parsley-family herb.

Chèvre [French] *(SHEVruh)*: Any cheese made from goat's milk.

Chianti [Italian] *(keAHNte)*: A dry, red table wine.

Chicharrones [Latin-American]: Crispy deep-fried pork skins, stewed in red or green chili sauce, or eaten as a snack similar to potato chips.

Chicken Florentine: Chicken topped with baby shrimp on a bed of spinach.

Chicken masaman curry [Thai-Thailand]: Chicken with *avocado* and cashew nuts in a highly seasoned and aromatic *curry*.

Chicken steak: A thin cut of inexpensive beef that is tenderized by pounding, dipped in a milk-egg mixture and then seasoned flour, and fried like chicken. Usually served with country gravy. Popular in the South and Midwest.

Chickory: A plant the leaves of which are used in salads, and the root of which is roasted and ground as a substitute for or an additive to coffee.

Chicote [Nicaraguan]**:** Charbroiled barbequed pork ribs.

Chiffonade: A mixture of finely cut vegetables, herbs or the like, for use in soups, salads, etc.

Chiktay Aranso [Haitian]**:** Smoked herring, *avocado*, pepper and onion salad.

Chimichanga [Mexican]**:** A burrito (a flat *tortilla*, which is made of unleavened bread) that is fried or deep-fried, with any number of fillings – shredded meat, grated cheese, refried beans and rice, *garnished* with shredded cheese, sour cream and salsa (sauce).

Chipotle [Mexican]**:** A pungent red pepper.

Chitterlings: The small intestines of animals, usually freshly slaughtered pigs. Popular in southern cooking.

Chive: The smallest member of the onion family, commonly chopped and sprinkled as a flavoring *garnish* on soups, salads, etc.

Chop suey [Chinese]: Translates as "mixed up". Americanized dish of many vegetables *sautéed*.

Chorizo (also Choriso) [Spanish]: Pork sausage spiced with garlic, peppers, and juniper berries and smoked and dried.

Choucroute [French]: Translates as "sauerkraut". Cabbage cooked with goose fat, onions, juniper berries and white wine, and served as a side or main dish. Choucroute garni is served with potatoes and a variety of meats – sausages, pork, ham or goose.

Chow mein [Chinese]: A highly Americanized dish of *sautéed* noodles with vegetables and spices.

Chuletas de Cordero [Spanish]: Lamb chops.

Churrasco [Spanish]: Grilled flank steak.

Churrasco de mero [Spanish]: Grilled grouper steak.

Churros [Latin-American]: Rope-shaped, sugar-dusted donut-like cakes, as popular as donuts.

Chutney [East Indian]: A sauce or relish made with fruit, herbs and spices.

Cilantro [Spanish]: *Coriander.*

Cioppino [Italian]: A stew of fish, shellfish, tomatoes and seasonings.

Cipollini *(chipoLEne)*: Bittersweet bulbs of the grape hyacinth, which taste and look like small onions.

Ciruela [Mexican]: Plum and **sherry** sauce.

Cognac [French] *(CONyac)*: French **brandy**, the finest of all the brandies.

Colada de cafe [Spanish]: Espresso coffee to go – an amount for a few people (comes with some very small paper cups).

Com chien [Vietnamese]: Fried rice with any or a combination of meats.

Compote [French]: Fruit stewed or cooked with a syrup, usually served as a dessert.

Concasse: Peeled, seeded and chopped tomato.

Conch *(CONk)*: The meat of a large spiral mollusk found in the Mediterranean.

Conch fritter *(CONk)*: Corn meal batter with minced conch, onions and spices, formed into a small round-to-oblong shape and deep-fried.

Condiment: A savory, piquant, spicy or salty accompaniment to food, such as ketchup and mustard.

Conejo con ciruelas [Spanish] *(conAho)*: Rabbit prepared with a prune sauce.

Confit: Pieces of meat cooked in their own fat and then stored in a pot covered with the fat. Also fruits and vegetables that have been cooked with sugar until jamlike.

Consommé: A clear soup which is the product of long, slow cooking.

Continental breakfast: A light meal of juice, coffee and rolls.

Coq au vin [French]**:** This classic French dish contains pieces of chicken, mushrooms, onions, bacon or salt pork and various herbs, cooked in red wine.

Coquilles St. Jacques [French] *(KohKEL sahn ZHAHK)***:** An appetizer of minced or whole scallops, oysters and/or clams in a wine and cream sauce topped with grated cheese and browned under a broiler; usually served in scallop shells.

Coriander: An herb of the parsley family (Spanish: cilantro).

Corn salad: A plant (not corn) with tender leaves that have a tangy, nutlike flavor. Native to Europe but grows well in the U.S. Considered a gourmet green, used raw in salads or steamed as a vegetable.

Cortadito [Spanish]**:** A small-size espresso coffee with milk.

Corvina [Spanish]**:** Sea bass.

Coulis *(kooLE)***:** A thick **puree** or sauce.

Couscous [North African]**:** Steamed **seminola** served with vegetables and meats.

Cozze [Italian]: Clam.

Creme brulee [French] *(krem broolay)*: Custard made with cream and eggs, topped by a layer of **caramel**.

Crème fraîche [French] *(krem fresh)*: Slightly fermented cream that has been thickened by lactic acids and natural fermentation.

Creole: A style of cooking that reflects the full-flavored combination of the best of French, Spanish and African cuisines. The emphasis is on cream and butter, rather than the pork fat that is used in **Cajun cuisine**.

Crepe: A thin, delicate pancake.

Crepe suzette [French] *(crape)*: A light pancake served rolled up or folded over in an orange sauce, sprinkled with an orange-based liquour or **brandy** and **flambéed** at table.

Crespelle [Italian] *(kresPELLay)*: Thin pancakes that are either stacked with different fillings between the layers or filled and rolled like **crepes**.

Crevette [French]: Shrimp.

Croissant: A rich, crescent-shaped bread roll.

Croqueta [Spanish} *(croKETa)*: A small cake or ball of meat, rice and/or vegetables, coated with egg and bread crumbs and fried in deep fat.

Crostini [Italian]: Small rounds of toasted or fried bread topped with a wide range of foods – cheese, *pâté*, *anchovy* paste, etc., usually served hot as *antipasto*.

Croûte fromage [French] *(cruTAY froMAZH)*: Toasted bread slices *glazed* with white wine and cheese.

Crouton: A small piece of toasted or fried bread, sometimes seasoned, used as a *garnish* for soups, salads or other dishes.

Crudité: Raw vegetables or fruits served as an *hors d'oeuvre*, generally cut into thin strips and served with a dip or sauce.

Cumin: A herb of the parsley family, particularly popular in Middle-Eastern, Asian and Mediterranean cooking, as in chili powders and curries.

Curry: Curry powder is a pulverized blend of up to 20 spices, herbs and seeds, used in any number of hot, spicy, gravy-based dishes of East Indian origin.

Daiquiri [West Indies]: An iced cocktail of rum, lime juice, sugar and fruit, such as banana, *papaya* or *mango*, processed in a blender.

Deditos [Spanish] *(daDEtos)*: Meat or cheese cut into thin strips.

Degustate

Degustate: To taste or savor.

Delmonico steak (Club steak)**:** A beefsteak cut from the rib end of the short loin, or sometimes a porterhouse or t-bone steak from which the *tenderloin* has been trimmed.

Demi-glace [French]**:** A strong coffee in a small cup, usually served after dinner, comparable to the Italian/Cuban espresso.

Dentice [Italian]**:** Red *snapper*, the most popular of the snapper varieties, a fish the flesh of which is firm-textured and contains very little fat.

Desayuno [Spanish]**:** Breakfast.

Dijón [French]**:** A medium-hot mustard.

Dill: An herb, the leaves of the dill plant, used to flavor a wide variety of foods, usually salads and vegetables.

Dim sum [Chinese]**:** Cantonese for "heart's delight", dim sum includes a variety of small, mouthwatering snacks such as steamed or fried dumplings, shrimp rolls, steamed buns and pastries.

Ding [Chinese]**:** Cut vegetables.

Dolmades [Greek]**:** An appetizer. Stuffed grape leaves, *blanched* and then wrapped around a filling, usually cooked rice and herbs, sometimes with meat, such as minced lamb, blanched, and served cold.

Dolphin (Mahi-Mahi): Called *mahi-mahi* so as not to be confused with the dolphin that is a mammal. A moderately fat fish with firm, flavorful flesh.

Dover (Channel) sole: A delicately flavored fish with a firm texture found in coastal waters from Denmark to the Mediterranean sea.

Du jour [French]: That which is served on a particular day.

Duck sauce [Chinese]: A sweet, pungent sauce that resembles *chutney*.

Eclair *(e-CLAIR)*: A usually chocolate-frosted oblong cream puff with whipped cream or custard filling.

Egg drop soup [Chinese]: Chicken broth with corn-starch and egg dropped into the steaming liquid.

Egg foo young [Chinese]: Small pancake-size portions of fried egg topped with various foods, such as bean sprouts, water chestnuts, scallions, ham, chicken or pork, and gravy.

Egg roll [Oriental]: Egg dough rolled into small oblong shape, filled with minced onions, carrots, cabbage, and meat, and deep fried.

Eggs Benedict: Eggs on English muffin and Canadian ham, with *hollandaise* sauce.

Elena Ruiz [Cuban]: A traditional Cuban sandwich of turkey, cream cheese, and strawberry preserves.

Emmentaler cheese: A nutty-sweet, mellow-flavored cheese from Switzerland.

Empanada [Latin-America]: A turnover or mold of pastry with various fillings, usually baked or fried.

Empanada gallega [Spanish] *(guyAguh)*: Meat or fish pie.

Empanizado [Spanish]: Breaded (as with **chicken steak**) and fried.

Emulsion: A mixture of one liquid with another with which it cannot combine smoothly, oil and water being the classic example.

En croûte [French] *(on KRUT)*: A dish served in a crust.

Enchilada [Mexican]: A **tortilla** on which meat filling is spread and which is rolled up and covered with chili-seasoned tomato sauce.

Endive [Belgian-French]: A lettuce-like plant with a slightly bitter flavor. The three types: Belgian, curly, and **escarole**.

Enoki mushroom (Enokitake): A crispy, delicate mushroom with long, spaghetti-like stems and tiny, snowwhite heads.

Enraged: Strongly spicy.

Ensalada [Spanish}: Salad.

Entrecôte marchand de vin [French]: Sautéed rib steak *garnished* with butter mixed with *shallots* and red wine.

Entrecôte sauté marchand de vin [French]: **Sautéed** rib steak (the term entrecôte refers to a steak cut between the ninth and eleventh ribs of beef) made with red wine, cream, beef stock and *shallots*.

Entree: A dish served as the main course of a meal. In parts of Europe, it is the dish served between the fish and meat courses in a formal dinner.

Escabeche [Spanish]: *Poached* or fried fish, covered with a spicy *marinade*. Usually served cold as an appetizer. Popular in Spain, parts of France, and Latin-America.

Escalope *(ehSKALohp)*: A thin, boneless slice of white meat, usually fried.

Escargot [French] *(escarGO)*: An edible snail.

Escargots Bourguignonne [French] *(escarGO boorgeeNYON)*: Snails in garlic butter sauce.

Escarole: A type of the lettuce-like endive plant with a mildly bitter flavor.

Escovitch [Jamaican]: Cooked fish pickled in a vinegar *marinade*.

Espresso con panna

Espresso con panna: Espresso coffee with whipped cream.

Essence: A distillation or diffusion of a substance which contains its characteristic properties in concentrated form.

Étouffee [Cajun] *(atuFAY)*: Shrimp or crawfish in a rich, spicy sauce over rice.

Evian: Non-carbonated bottled water.

Extra virgin olive oil: Olive oil made from the first pressing of highest-quality olives.

Fagioli [Italian]: The italian word for beans, usually white kidney beans.

Fajitas [Mexican] *(faHEtas)*: Seasoned and grilled strips of steak, chicken or seafood served with *tortilla*, *avocado*, shredded *cheddar cheese*, shredded lettuce, and peppers.

Falafel [Mediterranean]: A spicy bean mixture fried in vegetable oil and topped with *tahini* sauce.

Farfalle pasta: Pasta shaped like small butterflies or bow ties.

Fassoulada [Greek]: A soup of navy beans, olive oil, vegetables (usually carrots), garlic, onion, celery and seasonings.

Fatouch (Fattush) [Mediterranean]: Toasted bits of **pita** bread combined with tomatoes, cucumbers, green peppers, parsley, green onions, herbs and spices, and lemon dressing.

Fava bean: A tan, rather flat bean that resembles a large lima bean, usually sold dried or cooked and canned.

Fennel: An herb of the parsley family, the leaves and seeds of which are used for a flavoring, similar to **anise** but sweeter and more delicate.

Feta cheese [Greek]: A soft, white, brine-cured cheese made from sheep's or goat's milk, with a rich, tangy flavor.

Fettuccine [Italian] *(fetuCHEne)*: Pasta cut in flat narrow strips.

Fettuccine Alfredo [Italian] *(fetuCHEne)*: Fettuccine (flat, narrow strips of pasta) in a cream sauce, topped with **parmesan** cheese.

Fagottini [Italian]: Steamed pockets of romaine lettuce leaves wrapped around a mixture of seasonal vegetables, **parmesan** cheese, egg and breadcrumbs.

Fideos [Spanish]: Very thin, **vermicelli**-type pasta.

Filet mignon [French] *(fil A min YON)*: A small, tender round of steak cut from the thick end of a beef tenderloin.

Filo (phyllo): Extremely thin, almost transparent pastry sheets.

Fisch-klosschen [German]: Baked fish dumplings.

Flambé [French] *(flambA)*: Food served in flaming liquor, especially **brandy**.

Flan [Spanish]: A dessert of sweetened egg custard with a **caramel** topping.

Flauta [Mexican]: Any mixture of meat, vegetables and spices rolled up in a **tortilla**.

Florentine [Italian]· A dish prepared with spinach.

Focaccia [Italian] *(foCAchia)*: A large, round, flat bread sprinkled before baking with olive oil, salt and spices.

Foie gras [French] *(fwa grah)*: "Fat liver". The over-size liver of geese or ducks that have been force-fed to fatten them, often flavored with **truffles**.

Fondant: Sweets made from a paste produced by boiling sugar syrup and then kneading until it is soft, creamy and smooth.

Fondue: Originally a Swiss dish in which cheese is melted in a pot with white wine and flavorings and into which chunks of meat, bread or fruit are dipped with long-handled forks and eaten.

Fontina: A firm cow's milk cheese with a mild, nutty flavor.

Foon shee [Chinese]: Bean threads – also called **cellophane** noodles, made from bean flour.

Foon Woon Gal [Chinese]: Breaded and deep-fried chicken.

Foul mudamas [Mediterranean]: Fava beans blended with garlic and lemon, topped with vegetables and olive oil.

Fraise: Strawberry.

Framboise [French] *(framBWAZ)*: Raspberry. Also, a **brandy** distilled from raspberries.

Frijole [Spanish] *(freHOle)*: Bean.

Frijoles negros [Spanish *(freHOles)*: Black beans.

Frijoles refritos [Mexican]: Cooked beans, usually red or pinto beans, that are mashed and then fried.

Frisée [French] *(frisAY)*: Curly **endive**.

Fritata [Italian]: An omelet that usually has the ingredients mixed with the eggs rather than folded inside in the French style.

Fritter: Portions of food – fruit, vegetables, meat, seafood – coated in batter and deep-fried.

Fritto misto [Italian]: Italian for "mixed fry", fritto misto is a selection of bite-size pieces of meat, fish, or vegetables, dipped in a batter and deep-fried.

Frutti di mare [Italian]: Fruit of the sea – any sea food.

Fumé blanc wine: A variety of *sauvignon blanc*, an elegant dry wine.

Fusilli [Italian]: Pasta in the form of little spindles.

Futomaki roll [Japanese]: A type of *California (Sushi)* roll made of cucumber, crab, *avocado* and egg.

Gado gado [Indonesia]: A mixture of raw and slightly cooked vegetables served with a spicy peanut sauce made from hot chili peppers and coconut milk.

Gaelic steak [Irish]: A sirloin steak with a whiskey and mushroom sauce.

Gal ding [Chinese]: Stir fry with chicken chunks and vegetables.

Gal massaman [Thai]: Chicken in a sweet sauce with coconut milk and peanuts.

Gal pad kaprow [Thai]: Chicken seasoned with **basil** and chilies.

Gal sarm ros [Thai-Thailand]: Boneless chicken topped with a three-flavored sauce.

Galangal [Thai-Thailand]: A Chinese plant whose dried root has a gingery-peppery taste, much valued as a flavoring in East Asian cooking.

Galette [French]: A round, flat cake made of pastry or other types of dough and served with a wide variety of toppings.

Gambas [Philippine]: Olive oil, garlic, pickle and hot pepper sauté for seafood.

Gamberoni [Italian]: Shrimp.

Gang garee [Thai-Thailand]: The most familiar Thai **curry**: chicken in a golden curry sauce with potatoes and pineapple.

Garam masala [Indian-India]: A standard mixture of ground spices used in Indian cooking, commonly cinnamon, **cardamom**, cloves, **cumin**, **coriander**, and pepper.

Garnish: A decorative, edible accompaniment to finished dishes, from appetizers to desserts.

Gaufrette chips (wafers): Thin, slightly sweet, fan-shaped wafers, usually served with such desserts as ice cream and **mousse**.

Gazpacho [Spanish]: A soup made of chopped tomatoes, cucumbers, onions, and garlic, with oil and vinegar – served cold.

Gebratene ente [German]: Roast duck filled with apple-sausage stuffing.

Gefilte fish [Jewish]: A popular dish made of ground fish (usually *carp*, *pike* or *whitefish*) mixed with eggs, *matzo* meal and seasonings, formed into balls, and simmered.

Gemelli: Pasta in the form of twins.

Gerolsteiner: Naturally carbonated bottled water.

Ginger: A reed-like plant having a pungent, spicy flavor used in cookery.

Glaceau: Non-carbonated bottled water.

Glaze: Substance (usually sugar or sugar syrup) used to coat a food.

Gnocchi [Italian] *(NOche)*: Small dumplings made either from flour, *seminola*, or potato starch, boiled, baked, or grilled.

Gobi root [Japanese]: Slender root vegetable with a rusty brown skin and grayish-white flesh. Also called *burdock*.

Goong pad preau wan [Thai]: Sweet and sour shrimp or other seafood.

Gordita [Mexican]: Cornmeal pockets stuffed with ground beef, shredded cheese, diced potatoes, and sauce.

Gorgonzola cheese [Italian]: Sharp-flavored blue-veined creamy cow's milk cheese.

Gouda cheese: A pale yellow cheese, mild in flavor, in a flat round shape and often given a protective coating of wax.

Grand Marnier [French] *(marn YEA)*: A brand of liqueur having a **brandy** base and an orange flavor.

Gratinate (Gratiné) [French]: To bake or broil food in *au gratin* style (topped with browned bread crumbs or cheese).

Gravad laks (Gravlax) [Scandinavian]: Salmon marinated with *dill*.

Griglia [Italian]: A *marinade* for chicken prepared with lemon, *rosemary*, olive oil, and balsamic *vinegar*.

Grujo [Haitian]: Fried pork with *plantain*.

Gruyère cheese [French]: A firm pale-yellow cheese made of whole milk and having small holes.

Guacamole [Mexican] *(guacaMOlee)*: Mashed *avocado*, finely chopped onion and tomato, *cilantro*, lime juice, salt and green chili, served as a dip, sauce, topping or side dish.

Guava: Round to pear-shaped subtropical fruit, used in making jelly.

Gulab jamun [Indian-India]: Sweet fried pastry balls with honey syrup and rose water.

Gulaschsuppe [German]: A hearty beef-based soup with potatoes, vegetables and seasonings, especially paprika.

Gumbo [Creole]: A mélange of okra, vegetables, seafood, and sometimes sausage.

Gyoza [Japanese]: A meat-filled dumpling.

Gyro [Greek]: A Greek specialty consisting of minced lamb that is moulded around a spit and vertically roasted. The meat is usually sliced, wrapped in *pita* bread and topped with grilled onions, sweet peppers and a cucumber-yogurt sauce.

Ha gow [Chinese]: Steamed shrimp dumpling appetizer.

Habañero pepper: Small, lantern-shaped extremely hot chili pepper.

Halibut: Either of two large flatfishes, with a low-fat, white, firm and mild-flavored flesh.

Hamanabe [Japanese]: The Japanese have their own version of the French seafood soup bouillabaisse. Hamanabe is made with a variety of fish and shellfish and vegetables in soybean broth.

Hamantaschen [Jewish]: Small triangular pastries with a sweet filling, either of honey-poppy-seed, prune or apricot. A traditional sweet of Purim, a festive Jewish holiday.

Hamburguesa [Spanish]: Hamburger.

Har kew [Chinese]: Whole shrimp stirfry with vegetables.

Haricots verts [French]: Green beans (string beans).

Haseinusstorte [German]: Hazelnut sponge cake topped with sweetened whipped cream.

Helado [Spanish]: Ice cream.

Hibachi: A small Japanese-style charcoal *brazier* covered with a grill, usually used for outdoor cooking.

Hiyashi wakame [Japanese]: Crunchy spicy sesame seaweed salad.

Hiziki [Japanese]: A type of seaweed.

Hoisin (Peking) sauce [Chinese]: A thick, sweet and spicy reddish-brown sauce, a combination of *soybeans*, garlic, chili peppers and various spices.

Hollandaise sauce: A sauce of egg yolks, butter, lemon juice, and seasonings. May be served with *Eggs Benedict*, vegetables, or fish.

Hominy: An original American Indian food – dried white or yellow corn kernels from which the hull and germ have been removed.

Horiatiki salata [Greek]**:** Country-style salad, known in the U.S. as Greek salad, which features black olives and crumbled *feta* cheese.

Hors d'oeuvres: Small, usually one-or-two-bite size, appetizers served before a meal, customarily with *apértifs* or cocktails.

Horseradish: The pungent root of a plant of the mustard family, ground and used as a *condiment*.

Hot and sour soup [Chinese]**:** Shredded meat and vegetables in a spicy seasoned broth.

Huevo [Spanish]**:** Egg.

Huevos rancheros [Mexican]**:** Fried eggs served on *tortillas* (corn or flour pancake-shaped bread) with tomato sauce and seasonings.

Hummus [Middle Eastern]: Chickpea *puree* seasoned with sesame or garlic oil, garlic, lemon, and salt, usually eaten with *pita* bread.

Hush puppies [The U.S. South]: A small cornmeal dumpling flavored with onion and spices, deep-fried and served hot, usually with seafood, preferably fried catfish.

Hussaini Kabob [Indian-India]: Boneless cubes of lamb *marinated* in yogurt, garlic and *ginger*, *skewered* and roasted in a clay oven *(tandoori)*.

Indian pudding [New England]: A pudding consisting of cornmeal, molasses, milk, eggs, butter and sweet spices, such as *ginger*, cinnamon and vanilla flavoring.

Infuse: To introduce, usually by pouring a liquid.

Insalata di Mare [Italian]: Seafood salad.

Jaiba [Spanish] *(HAi bah)*: Blue crab.

Jalapeño [Spanish] *(halaPENyo)*: A hot green or orange-red pepper.

Jambalaya [Creole]: One of *Creole* cookery's high-lights, combining rice with a variety of ingredients, such as vegetables, shellfish, meat and spices, depending upon the cook.

Jardinière [French]: A dish *garnished* with vegetables.

Java: Slang word for coffee.

Jerk flavoring [Caribbean]: Pork, chicken or any food rubbed with chilies, herbs and spices.

Jicama [Mexican] *(HEkamah)*: The large edible tuberous root of a tropical plant, eaten as a vegetable either raw or boiled.

Jugo de melocoton [Spanish] *(ugo de melocoTON)*: Peach nectar.

Jugo de naranja [Spanish] *(ugo de naranha)*: Orange juice.

Jugo de toronja [Spanish] *(ugo de toRONuh)*: Grapefruit.

Julienne [French]: Vegetables cut into thin strips. Also, a clear soup *garnished* with julienne vegetables.

Jus de poulet [French]: A concentrated chicken jelly, obtained by a series of *reductions*.

Kabrit nan sos [Haitian]: Goat stewed in tomato sauce with rice.

Kaeng kew wan [Thai]: *Curried* meat, fish or poultry.

Kaeng kew wan nuer [Thai]**:** Sliced beef in green *curry* sauce (very spicy), with eggplant, coconut milk, chilies, lime leaves and *basil*.

Kaeng phed [Thai]**:** Fish, chicken or meat in a red *curry* sauce (medium spicy).

Kalamarakia [Greek]**:** An appetizer: bite-size batter-dipped and fried squid.

Kalamata olives: A purple-black olive, often slit to allow the wine-vinegar *marinade* in which it is soaked to penetrate the flesh.

Kaibi [Korea]**:** Barbecued beef ribs.

Kao pad [Thai]**:** Stir-fried rice with a variety of vegetables.

Kappa [Japanese]**:** Cucumber and seasoned rice rolled in seaweed.

Kartoffelcremesuppe [German]**:** Cream of potato soup made with chicken stock, onion and cream.

Kartoffelpuffer [German]**:** Potato pancakes.

Kassler ripchen [Bavarian]**:** Smoked pork chops, broiled and served over *sauerkraut*.

Katsu [Japanese]**:** A form of breading, used with chicken, fish and beef.

Kavakia [Greek]**:** Seafood soup.

Kebab

Kebab (Shish Kebab) [Turkish]: Cubes of meat (as lamb or beef) *marinated* and cooked with vegetables (as onions, tomatoes and green peppers) on a *skewer*.

Keema matar [Indian-India]: Minced meat cooked with green peas, ginger and onions.

Kefta [Mediterranean]: Fresh ground lamb and beef mixed with parsley and onions, seasoned, and charbroiled.

Key lime [Florida Keys]: A small yellow lime with a bitter rather than sour taste.

Kheer [Indian-India]: Rice pudding made with rich thick milk, *garnished* with almonds, raisins and pistachios.

Kibbeh [Mediterranean]: Seasoned ground beef mixed with crushed wheat, onions and pine nuts and fried.

Kim chee (Kim chi) [Korean]: A spicy pickled or fermented mixture of ingredients, such as fish and vegetables.

Kishka [Jewish]: Sausage made with beef and spices.

Kiwi *(KEYwe)*: A vivid green-fleshed fruit flecked with black seeds, used often for its decorative appearance.

Knish [Jewish]: *Crêpe* made with spinach or potato and baked.

Knockwurst [Jewish] *(NAHKworst)*: Sausage made with beef and spices.

Kota kapama [Greek]: Chicken pieces sautéed with vegetables in a tomato-onion sauce flavored with cinnamon, served on a bed of pasta.

Kourabledes [Greek]: Traditional Greek butter cookies.

Kumquat: A small round or oblong citrus fruit having a sweet rind and acid pulp, used chiefly for preserves.

Kung pao (gung pao) [Chinese]: Chicken with peanuts and hot peppers.

Kushi-Katsu [Japanese]: Meat (chicken, fish, beef) dipped in katsu (batter) and deep-fried on a skewer.

"Do you call __this__ Kushi-Katsu?"

L'Insalata di "giullo" [Italian]: *Caesar* salad.

La fricassee de crevettes cannoise [French] *(canWAZ)*: *Sautéed* shrimps in cream sauce with crab meat and green and red peppers.

La terrine [French]: *Mousse* of duck liver *pâté*.

Laap gai [Thai-Thailand]: A spicy chicken appetizer, served with a salad.

Labneh (Lebneh) [Mediterranean]: Condensed yogurt served with olive oil, tomatoes and mint *garnish*.

Laksa [Malaysian]: Spiced noodle soup – a Malaysian national dish

Lanbi boukannen [Haitian]: Conch in sauce with yam.

Langosta [Spanish]: Lobster.

Lasagna [Italian] *(laZANyuh)*: Broad, flat noodles. Also, lasagna baked, usually with meat, cheese and tomato sauce.

Latke [Jewish]: Crisp pancakes made from grated potatoes.

Le dauphin aux poireaux [French] *(la douFAN o poirO)*: Filet of *dolphin (mahi-mahi)* in *leek* sauce.

Le feuilletee d'escargots [French] *(le fuhyuh TAHZ de escargo)*: an **hors d'oeuvre**: snails in pastry shell with **cognac** sauce.

Le filet wellington [French] *(le filA)*: **Filet mignon** in a pastry shell with **périgourdine** sauce.

Le saumon fume de norvege [French]: **Hors d'oeuvre**: smoked salmon with **capers**, chopped onions on toast.

Lechon [Spanish] *(laeCHON)*: Pork.

Lechuga [Spanish]: Lettuce.

Leek: The national vegetable of Wales – related to the garlic and onion, with a milder fragrance and flavor.

Legim [Haitian]: Vegetable stew with white rice and red bean sauce.

Lentil: A small bean of European origin, often used in soups. A good source of vitamins A and B, iron, and phosphorus.

Les coeurs de palmiers cardinal [French] *(luh cour da PALmeur)*: Appetizer: Hearts of palm in a beet-flavored **vinaigrette**.

Les escalopes de saumon à la royale [French] *(luh esKALup)*: Fresh salmon filet with spinach in **Hollandaise** sauce.

Les escalopes de veau vailee [French]
(luh esKALup day vo vaLAY): Veal scalopini in calvados and mushroom sauce.

Lingonberry: Mountain cranberry.

Linguine [Italian]: Long, flat, slender pasta strips.

Lo mein [Chinese]: Soft noodles *parboiled* and added to a meat-vegetable mixture.

Lobster Cantonese [Chinese]: Stir-fried lobster in the shell with a seasoned black bean sauce.

Lombardia [Italian]: Creamy pink *gorgonzola* sauce for pasta.

Lomito de cerdo asada [Spanish]: Roast pork loin.

Lychee: A small fruit with a bright red shell and creamy white flesh that is juicy and delicately sweet; commonly eaten as a snack, in fruit salad, or as a dessert. Much favored in the Orient.

Ma po [Chinese]: *Wok*-cooked *tofu* with ground pork, *ginger*, garlic, hot chili peppers, and *soy* sauce.

Ma po bean tofu [Chinese]: A vegetable dish of *braised* fresh bean curd cubes with chopped mushrooms, water chestnuts, ground pork, garlic, *ginger*, chili paste and scallions.

Macadamia nut: The fruit of an Australian evergreen tree, most commonly found salted and bottled.

Macrobiotic: An Orient-based health food diet of salt and sugar free, vegetarian, whole-grain recipes.

Madeira wine *(muhDEERuh)*: A rich, strong white or amber wine resembling *sherry*.

Maharaja patiala korma [Indian-India]: An ancient Indian recipe... bonless chicken blended with almonds, cashews, *ginger* and garlic.

Mahi-mahi: A type of *dolphin* fish called mahi-mahi so as not to confuse it with the dolphin mammals. Moderately fat with firm, flavorful flesh.

Maître d' butter: Melted butter with lemon juice or vinegar, chopped parsley and seasonings served with meat, fish or poultry.

Malanga: A large, firm root vegetable with a brown skin and white flesh, found in Latin America and the Caribbean.

Malt: Soluble powder made of dehydrated milk and malted cereals.

Manchego cheese [Spanish]: A rich, golden semi-firm cheese that has a full, mellow flavor.

Mandarin [Chinese]: A more hot and spicy cooking style than the usual Chinese recipes.

Mandarin pancakes

Mandarin pancakes [Chinese]: A pancake used for wrapping a variety of foods.

Mandelschnitzel [German]: Boneless chicken breast breaded with ground almonds and *sautéed* with raisins.

Mandu [Korean]: Dumplings.

Mango: Variously sized and shaped sweet fruit of a tropical tree, which has a fragrant and delectable golden flesh.

Manicotti [Italian]: A dish consisting of large, tubular noodles stuffed with a mild cheese and baked in a tomato sauce.

Manish water [Jamaican]: Highly seasoned goat soup.

Marinade: A seasoned liquid (vinegar, wine, etc.) with oil, herbs and spices in which meat, fish or vegetables are steeped before cooking.

Marinara: A highly seasoned sauce of tomatoes, garlic and spices.

Mariquitas [Spanish] *(maruhKEYtas)*: Fried green *plantain* chips.

Mariscada [Spanish]: Shellfish in garlic sauce.

Marjolaine: The French word for the herb marjoram. Also, a long, rectangular meringue dessert, nut-flavored and filled with sweetened whipped cream.

Marjoram: An aromatic small-leaved herb which varies from sweet to mild and pungent.

Marrow: A soft, fatty vascular tissue in the interior cavities of bones, used in many types of recipes.

Marsala wine: A sweet, dark, fortified wine, the flavor varying from sweet to dry.

Masaman curry [Thai-Thailand]: *Avocado* and cashew nuts in a highly seasoned and aromatic *curry*.

Mascarpone cheese [Italian]: A sweet, buttery, ivory-colored soft and delicate cheese.

Masitas de pollo [Spanish] *(POYo)*: Boneless chicken breast nuggets.

Matzo (matzoh) [Jewish]: A thin, brittle unleavened bread, traditionally eaten during the Jewish Passover holiday.

Matzo balls [Jewish]: *Matzo* meal balls made with oil, eggs, and spices, and boiled, as in matzo ball soup.

Medallion: a small, coin-shaped piece of meat, usually beef, veal, or pork.

Media krassata [Greek]: Mussels cooked in wine sauce and served on a bed of rice.

Mee grob [Thai-Thailand]: Appetizer: crispy rice noodles cooked with shrimp and vegetables.

Melange: Mixture.

Melanzane [Italian]: Eggplant.

Merlot wine: A dark red wine, similar in flavor to cabernet sauvignon, but tends to be softer and more mellow.

Mesclun [French]: A type of salad consisting of an assortment of different leaves, such as *endive*, lettuce, dandelion, *arugula*, etc.

Mesquite *(mesKEET)*: Used in grilling and smoking meats, mesquite wood gives off a slightly sweet smoke.

Meunière [French] *(muhnYAIR)*: Food cooked lightly coated in flour, fried in butter, and sprinkled with lemon juice, melted butter, and parsley.

Mezze: The word for appetizer in Greece and the Near East.

Mien ga [Vietnamese]: Chicken and cellophane noodle (also known as bean thread) soup.

Milanese: A cooking style originating in the Italian city of Milan, generally referring to food, usually meat, dipped in beaten egg, then into a breadcrumb-*parmesan* mixture and fried in butter.

Mille-feuille [French] *(meelFWEE)*: A cake, typically a small square one, made of layers of puff pastry, filled with cream.

Minestrone [Italian]: Minestrone, or "big soup", is a thick vegetable soup that usually contains pasta, peas, and/or beans. often topped with grated **parmesan** cheese – hearty enough to be a full meal.

Mirepoix (Mirepois) *(mihrPWAH)*: A mixture of diced carrots, onions, celery and herbs **sautéed** in butter, used to season sauces, soups and stews.

Mirin [Japanese]: An alcoholic drink, pale golden in color and sweet, made from fermented rice – essentially a sweeter version of **sake**. Used mainly in cooking.

Miso [Japanese]: Fermented soybean paste – a staple of Japanese cuisine.

Miso soup [Japanese]: Dashi (fish broth) with miso (fermented **soybean** paste), to which can be added a wide variety of meats and vegetables. In Japan it is a common breakfast food, but can be eaten at any meal.

Mongolian [Chinese]: Northern Chinese cuisine, featuring lamb, mutton, and yogurt.

Monkfish: Also known as **angler** fish and by other names. Low-fat and firm-textured, with a mild, sweet, lobster-like flavor.

Montmorency, á la: Made or served with cherries, applying to various desserts and entrees, as caneton á la Montmorency – roast duckling with cherry sauce.

Moo goo gai pan [Chinese]: Stir-fried chicken with button mushrooms and thickened white sauce.

Moo shi pork [Chinese]: Pork stir-fried with lily-buds, cloud ear mushrooms, and scrambled eggs.

Moo yang [Thai]: Grilled sliced pork with herbs, green peppercorns and lime juice.

Morel: An edible mushroom.

Moros [Spanish]: Rice and black beans cooked together.

Moussaka, also mousaka [Greek]: Sliced eggplant and ground lamb or beef that are layered and baked. There are endless preparation variations.

Mousse: A dessert of sweetened and flavored whipped cream, or thin cream and gelatin, frozen without stirring. Also, any preparation with a *mousse* consistency.

Mousse au chocolat [French]: A rich, light chocolate pudding-like dessert.

Moutarde [French]: Mustard.

Mozzarella cheese [Italian] *(mahtsuhRELuh)*: A white, mild-flavored cheese which in the U.S. is used primarily grated for pizza and toppings.

MSG (monosodium glutamate): A flavor enhancer, originating and most popular in China and Japan. Some people have reactions to MSG, such as flushing and burning sensations and headaches. For this reason, MSG is not widely used in the U.S.

Mu shu pork [Chinese]: Stir-fried scrambled eggs, shredded cabbage, bamboo shoots, lily buds, mushrooms and shredded pork, served with hoisin sauce (made with *soy* sauce and seasonings).

Muffuletta [New Orleans]: A sandwich made with a large round roll of Italian bread split in half and filled with layers of hard salami, ham, provolone, and olive salad.

Mulligatawny soup [Indian-India]: Delicately spiced vegetable soup.

Muesli *(MYOOSlee)*: A health food cereal, a mixture of grains, nuts, wheat germ, dried fruit, etc. Usually labeled granola in the U.S.

Nacatamal [Nicaraguan]: Corn meal *tamal* – ground meat seasoned usually with chili, rolled in cornmeal dough, wrapped in corn husks, and steamed.

Nachos: Nacho chips typically served with melted cheddar cheese, spicy picante sauce, sour cream and sliced *jalapeños*.

Nage

Nage (a la nage) [French]**:** A light white-wine-based vegetable stock in which small crustaceans are cooked.

Nam sod [Thai-Thailand]**:** Appetizer – spicy ground pork served on a green salad.

Napoleon: A rich pastry consisting of several oblong layers of puff pastry with a filling of cream custard or jelly, often topped with melted chocolate.

Nasi rames [Indonesian]**:** An *entree* consisting of a wide variety of meat, seafood and vegetables.

Natilla [Spanish] *(nuhTEyuh)*: Egg custard dessert.

Navarin [French]**:** Lamb or mutton stewed with vegetables, which vary according to the season. Spring Navarin would contain carrots, turnips, beans, peas, etc.

Nawabi Biryani [Indian-India]**:** Tender boneless pieces of lamb, goat, chicken and shrimp and vegetables cooked with spices, nuts and imported Indian rice in a special sauce.

Noodles Peking style [Chinese]**:** Boiled egg noodles and shredded cucumbers topped with a special richly-flavored sauce.

Nougat: Soft or hard chewy preparation of nuts, sugar, and honey.

Nova: Salmon prepared in the cold-smoked style.

Oktapodl skaras [Greek]: Octopus strips *marinated* in red wine, olive oil and seasonings, especially *oregano*, and grilled. Served with lemon wedges.

Opal basil: A form of *basil*, an herb of the mint family.

Orecchiette Pasta: Pasta in the form of small ears.

Oregano: A herb of the *marjoram* family, native of Italy and much used in Italian cuisine.

Orzo [Italian]: Pasta in the form of small ricelike grains.

Osso bucco [Italian]: Veal stew made of unboned pieces of veal braised in white wine with tomatoes, onions, leeks, and herbs and spices.

Ostiones [Spanish]: Oysters.

Oyster sauce [Chinese]: A sauce made of oyster extract, salt and spices – does not taste like oysters.

Oysters Rockefeller: Oysters spread with a mixture of spinach, butter, seasonings, and bread crumbs and baked on the half shell.

Pad Thai

Pad Thai [Thai-Thailand] *(pad tie)*: Rice noodles sautéed with shrimp, eggs, and vegetables.

Paella [Spanish] *(pieA Yuh)*: A dish prepared by **simmering** together chicken, seafood, rice, vegetables, with **saffron** and other seasonings.

Panang curry [Thai-Thailand]: Any meat with coconut milk, makrud leaves, vegetables, and special *curry*.

Pancetta: An Italian bacon that is cured with salt and spices but not smoked, formed into a sausage-like roll.

Paneer Bhurji [Indian-India]: Grated fresh home-made cheese cooked with green peas, green peppers, tomatoes and onions.

Papas fritas [Spanish]: French fries.

Papas hervidas [Spanish]: Boiled potatoes.

Papaya: The fruit of a semitropical American tree with large oblong yellow-when-ripe fruit, usually eaten raw, and has an exotic sweet-tart flavor. The fruit contains papain, a meat tenderizer.

Parboil: To boil briefly as a preliminary or incomplete procedure.

Parfait [French] *(parFA)*: A flavored custard containing whipped cream and syrup layers frozen without stirring.

Pargo [Spanish]: Red **snapper**.

Pargo a la tipitapa [Nicaraguan]: Deep fried whole red **snapper** topped with a special sweet and sour onion and tomato sauce.

Parillada [Spanish] *(pareeAHduh)*: Grilled.

Parma ham [Italian]: Ham from the city of Parma in Italy.

Parmesan cheese: A hard, dry cheese made from skimmed or partially skimmed cow's milk.

Parmigiani cheese [Italian]: Known in the U.S. as parmesan, a hard cow's milk cheese, usually grated.

Parrillada de carne [Spanish] *(paaareeAHda de CARne)*: Assorted grilled meats.

Pasilla chile [Spanish] *(pasEya)*: Both fresh (called chilaca) and dried (called pasilla), this pepper has a rich, hot flavor.

Passion fruit: A sweet fruit originating in Brazil, now also grown in semitropical areas. The fruit (so named because parts of the flowers represent symbols of Christ's crucifixion), is sweet-tart, the fragrance perfumy. The tiny black seeds are edible.

Pasta alla panna [Italian]: Pasta with a sauce of cream, butter, cheese and nutmeg.

Pasta Ripiena [Italian]: Stuffed pasta.

Pastel de key limon [Spanish]: *Key lime* pie.

Pastelles [Cuba and Puerto Rico]: A side dish of seasoned ground beef and masa (corn or grated *plantain* – cooking banana, dough) wrapped in plantain leaves or corn husks and boiled.

Pâté [French]: Seasoned ground meat that may be smooth or coarse in texture made from pork, veal, chicken, fish, liver and/or vegetables. Served either hot or cold, and possibly in pastry.

Pâté de fole gras [French] *(pahTA de FWAH GRAH)*: goose liver *pâté*.

Paw-paw (papaya): The fruit of a subtropical/tropical tree with large oblong yellow fruit, usually eaten raw.

Peaches melba: A dessert of peaches with raspberry sauce topped with whipped cream.

Pechuga de pollo [Spanish] *(POyo)*: Chicken breast.

Pecorino cheese [Italian]: Sheep's milk cheese, usually hard and dry, and good for grating and in cooking.

Peking (Beijing) [Chinese]: The site of the imperial court and therefore the most sophisticated of the regional cuisines – lightly seasoned, with much use of garlic.

Peking duck [Chinese]**:** Roasted duck with a golden, very crisp skin.

Pelan [Caribbean]**:** Rice cooked with meat, seafood or chicken, vegetables and seasonings.

Penne [Italian] *(PENae)***:** Large, straight tubes of macaroni cut on the diagonal.

Pepperpot [West Indian]**:** A soup or stew containing meat or seafood, vegetables, chili peppers, cassareep (a bittersweet **condiment**), **cayenne** pepper and other seasonings.

Périgourdine sauce [French]**:** Flavored with **truffles**.

Pescado a la Veracruzana [Mexican]**:** Whole fish, usually red **snapper**, cooked in a tomato sauce with olives, onions, garlic and chilies.

Pesce [Italian]**:** Fish.

Pesto [Italian]**:** A green aromatic pasta sauce of basil, **parmesan** cheese, garlic, olive oil, and often pine kernels or walnuts pounded into a paste.

Petit four [French] *(puh TEET)***:** A small, fancy cake, biscuit or sweet – such as a piece of crystallized or chocolate-covered fruit – typically served with coffee at the end of a meal.

Petto del pollo [Italian]**:** Boned chicken breast sautéed with sweet Italian sausage.

Pfeffer steak

Pfeffer steak [Bavarian] *(FEFer)*: Boneless sirloin *sautéed* with *shallots* and green peppercorns, topped with *Bordelaise* sauce.

Pho [Vietnamese]: Beef and noodle soup.

Phyllo (also filo): Extremely thin, almost transparent pastry sheets.

Picadillo [Spanish] *(peekahDEyo)*: A mixture of ground beef, eggs, and Spanish spices.

Piccata [Italian]: Meat, such as veal or chicken, that is seasoned and floured, quickly *sautéed*, and served with a sauce made from the pan drippings, lemon juice and chopped parsley.

Picka-peppa [Jamaican]: A *mango-tamarind* based spicy sauce.

Pike: A freshwater fish known for its lean, firm, low-fat but bony flesh – the common fish of French *quenelles* and Jewish *gefilte* fish.

Pikilla [Greek]: An assortment of hot and cold appetizers.

Pilaf [Persian and Turkish]: Rice usually combined with meat and vegetables, fried in oil, steamed in stock, and seasoned with any of numerous herbs, such as *saffron* and *curry*.

Piña colada [West Indies] *(peenyuh)*: Spanish for "strained pineapple" – a tropically-flavored iced drink made of coconut cream, pineapple juice and rum. The piña colada flavor has become popular for many uses such as ice cream and candy.

Pinot blanc: A light white wine originating in the Champagne region of France.

Pinot noir: A dry, red table wine of Burgundy type, produced in California from a purple Pinot grape.

Pisang bermadu [Malaysian]: Banana *fritters* with honey.

Pita bread: Also called pocket bread. Each pita round splits horizontally to form a pocket into which a variety of ingredients can be stuffed to make a sandwich.

Plantain: A large cooking banana with a mild, almost squash-like flavor.

Piat ak tout bagay [Haitian]: Appetizer sample platter.

Platano madino frito [Spanish]: Fried ripe plantains (cooking bananas).

Po boy (Poor boy): A form of hero sandwich – an oblong roll piled with meat, cheese, pickles, peppers – anything the cook is in the mood for. Its name reflects its status as cheap food for the poor.

Poach: To cook in a liquid kept just below the boiling point.

Poblano: A dark green chili pepper with a rich flavor that varies from mild to snappy, the darker the richer the flavor.

Poisson [French] *(pwahSOHN)*: Fish.

Polenta [Italian]: A thick mush of cornmeal, usually baked or fried.

Pollo [Spanish] *(POyo)*: Chicken.

Pollo a la barbacoa [Spanish] *(POyo)*: Barbecued chicken.

Pollo asado [Spanish] *(POyo)*: Roast chicken.

Pollo frito [Spanish] *(POyo)*: Fried chicken.

Pomodori secchi [Italian]: Sun-dried tomatoes.

Pomodoro [Italian]: Pasta sauce of fresh tomatoes, garlic and *basil*, *sautéed* in virgin olive oil.

Porcini [Italian]: A mushroom with a meaty texture and pungent, woodsy flavor.

Porcini: *Penne* pasta sauce prepared with porcini mushrooms.

Portobello: A large mushroom.

Portobello venezia [Italian]: Portobello mushroom topped with *provolone*, *prosciutto* ham and a red wine and rosemary sauce.

Posillipo [Italian]: A *marinara* sauce for seafood.

Postre [Spanish]: Dessert.

Pot-au-feu [French]: A variety of meat and vegetables (typically carrots, turnips, onions, *leeks* and celery) *simmered* long and slow in a large pot.

Potage [French]: Soup.

Potato latka [Jewish]: Ground white potato with egg and flour, fried in oil or deep-fried.

Potsticker: Small dumplings made of wonton skins filled with ground meat or shellfish, chopped water chestnuts, scallions and seasonings, browned on one side and then simmered in broth, usually served as an appetizer.

Poulet [French] *(pouLE)*: Chicken.

Prawn: A crustacean similar to, and sometimes used as synonymous with, shrimp.

Primavera [Italian]: Prepared with a variety of chopped or minced vegetables.

Pritikin style: Food that is steamed, with no oil.

Profiterole: A miniature cream puff made with a variety of fillings.

Prosciutto [Italian] *(proSHOOtoh)*: Dry-cured seasoned ham, usually sliced very thin.

Provençal

Provençal [French]: A dish cooked with garlic, onion, olive oil, mushrooms, and herbs.

Provolone [Italian]: A hard cow's-milk cheese.

Psari tis skaras [Greek]: Firm-fleshed white fish basted with olive oil, lemon juice and herbs, usually *oregano*, and baked, served with the remaining basting sauce.

Psari tsi skaras [Greek]: Grilled fish.

Pudin de pan [Spanish]: Bread pudding.

Pupu [Hawaiian]: The term for any hot or cold appetizer.

Pure de papas [Spanish]: Mashed potatoes.

Puree *(pyurA)*: Any food (usually a fruit or vegetable) that is finely mashed to a smooth, thick consistency.

Puttanesca [Italian]: A spicy red pasta sauce of capers, *kalamata* (also spelled calamata) olives and anchovy.

Pwason boirkannen [Haitian]: Grilled whole *snapper* with a tomato-scallion relish.

Quenelle: A dumpling of finely chopped fish or meat that is **poached** in water or stock (the strained liquid that is the result of cooking vegetables, meat or fish and other seasoning ingredients in water) and usually served with a sauce.

Quesadilla [Mexican] *(kasahDEya)*: A tortilla (Mexico's everyday bread – round and flat like a very thin pancake) folded over a filling of shredded cheese, onions and chilies and broiled or fried.

Queso [Spanish] *(KAYso)*: Cheese.

Quiche [French] *(KEYsh)*: A baked custard pie (usually not sweet) with an added savory ingredient, such as seafood, ham, or vegetables.

Quinos [Spanish] *(keNOuh)*: A tall crop plant of the goosefoot family, cultivated in Peru and Chile for its small, ivory-colored seed, which is used as a food staple.

Rable de lapin rissone [French]: Crisp, **sautéed saddle** of rabbit with white beans and baby **fennel**.

Radicchio [Italian]: A variety of **chicory** lettuce with a compact head of reddish, white-streaked leaves, usually found in salads.

Ragout

Ragout [French] *(raGOO)*: Meat and vegetables well-seasoned and cooked in a thick, rich, usually brown, sauce.

Rambutans [Thai-Thailand]: Thai fruit in light syrup.

Ramen soup [Japanese]: A soup made of noodles, small pieces of meat and vegetables, and broth.

Ramp: A wild onion, also called wild *leek*.

Ratatouille [French] *(ratuhTOOe)*: A stew of eggplant, tomatoes, green peppers, zucchini, onion and garlic, cooked in olive oil.

Ravioli [Italian]: Pasta in the form of small shells, stuffed with cheese, spinach and/or meat.

Reduction: A liquid (usually *stock*, wine or some other sauce mixture) boiled rapidly until the volume is reduced by evaporation, thereby thickening the consistency and intensifying the flavor.

Reggiano [Italian]: A high-quality *parmesan* cheese that is usually aged for several years before use.

Relleno [Mexican] *(rayENo)*: Stuffed, especially filled with cheese.

Rémoulade [French]: A pungent sauce or dressing resembling mayonnaise but usually made with cooked egg yolks and often with savory herbs or *condiments*.

Rendang Daging [Thai-Thailand]: Beef stewed in spiced coconut milk.

Repochetas [Nicaraguan]: Deep fried cheese-filled tortillas (round and flat unleavened bread).

Ricotta [Italian]: A rich fresh cheese – white, moist and with a slightly sweet flavor, somewhat grainy but smoother than cottage cheese.

Rigatoni [Italian]: A hollow pasta made in a short, curved, fluted shape.

Risotto [Italian]: Rice cooked in meat *stock* and seasoned in any of several ways, as with butter and cheese, or with wine and *saffron*.

Risotto nero [Italian]: Rice blended with squid ink and served with *calamari* or shrimp.

Rollmops [German]: Pickled herring rolls.

Romano cheese [Italian]: A hard cheese that is sharper than *parmesan*.

Ropa vieja [Spanish] *(veAha)*: Spanish for "old clothes" – the name of a dish consisting of seasoned shredded beef.

Rosemary: An herb – an evergreen shrub or the mint family.

Rotelle [Italian]: Small, round pasta that resembles a wheel with spokes.

Roti [West Indian]: Unleavened, crepe-like (thin pancake) bread wrapped around a *curry* filling.

Rotini [Italian]: Short pasta spirals.

Rotisserie: A cooking appliance fitted with a spit on which food is rotated before or over a source of heat.

Rouladen [German]: Round (less tender) steak rolled and stuffed with bacon, carrots and pickles, *braised* and *simmered* in its own gravy.

Roux [French] *(ROO)*: A blend of equal amounts of flour and butter, heated until the flour is cooked. It is used for thickening sauces.

Ruggulah [Jewish]: A Hanukkah tradition: bite-sized crescent-shaped cookies that can have a variety of fillings, such as fruit, nuts, poppy-seed cake, or jam.

Rumaki [Oriental]: A hot appetizer consisting of a strip of bacon wrapped around a slice of water chestnut and a bite-size piece of chicken liver that has been marinated overnight in a *soy* sauce-*ginger*-garlic mixture. The rumaki is skewered with a toothpick and grilled.

Saddle: A cut of meat taken from the part of an animal's body corresponding to where a saddle goes on a horse.

Saffron: A yellow-orange pungent, aromatic spice derived from the crocus flower. Saffron is the most expensive spice; each flower provides only three stigmas, which must be carefully hand-picked and then dried – an extremely labor-intensive process.

Sage: A mint-family herb with grayish-green pungent and aromatic leaves.

Sahnesauce hering [German]: An appetizer: pickled herring in sour cream with onions.

Sake [Japanese] *(SAke)*: A yellowish, slightly sweet wine (alcohol content 12 to 15 percent) made from fermented rice. Sake, the national alcoholic drink of Japan, is served warm in small porcelain cups.

Salade Melangee [French]: Mixed greens salad, usually served with the house vinaigrette: oil and vinegar, garlic, salt and black pepper.

Salpicon [Spanish]: Meat loaf.

Salsa [Mexican]: A sauce, especially a hot sauce containing chilies.

Salsiccia [Italian]: Sausage.

Salsify: A long, thin, white-fleshed root of the daisy family. Salsify is also known as oyster plant because its taste resembles a delicately flavored oyster.

Saltimbocca

Saltimbocca [Italian]: Saltimbocca, or "jump mouth", is a Roman specialty made of finely sliced veal sprinkled with **sage** and topped with a thin slice of prosciutto (Italian seasoned and salt-cured ham).

Sambal goreng udang [Indonesian]: Spicy hot and sweet **entree** of seafood cooked in a sauce of coconut milk, garlic and hot red chili.

San Peligrino: Non-carbonated bottled water.

Sancocho [West Indian]: A hearty soup or stew made with different root vegetables and squash, green plantain – cooking banana, yams, pumpkin and meat, such as pork or beef, and seasonings.

Sangria [Spanish]: A blend of wines, fruit juices and other spirits served chilled with fresh fruit over ice.

Sariwang Lumpia [Philippine]: Fresh egg roll.

Sashimi [Japanese]: Assorted filets of raw fish, **conch**, octopus.

Satay [Thai-Thailand]: Appetizer – sliced meat on a stick, charcoal broiled, and served with peanut and cucumber sauces.

Saucisson a lá tiede, salade de [French]: Warm garlic sausage, served on a green lentil salad.

Sauerbraten [German]: Eye round of beef **marinated** in red **burgundy** and herbs, roasted and served with gravy and potato dumpling.

Sauerkraut [German]: Shredded cooked pickled cabbage.

Sauté *(sawTA)*: To cook food quickly in a small amount of oil in a skillet or sauté pan over direct heat.

Sauterne: A usually semi-sweet golden-colored table wine.

Sauvignon blanc: A widely-cultivated grape that produces a grassy, herbaceous flavored dry wine of that name (also fumé blanc, and other varietal names).

Scaloppini: Thin slices of meat (such as veal) *sautéed* or coated with flour and fried.

Scampi: Sauce of fresh garlic, white wine, scallions and tomato – often served with shrimp.

Scarpariello [Italian]: A sauce for chicken containing Italian sausage, black olives, pepperoncini, Italian salami, and white wine.

Schnitzeltopf [German]: Veal stew with onions, mushrooms, cream and herbs.

Schwarzwälder bauernschinken [German]: An appetizer: smoked Westphalian ham (both cured and smoked, it is dark and has a mild, smoky taste), on slices of pumpernickel or rye bread.

Schwarzwälder kirschtorte [German]: Black forest cake.

Scotch bonnet: A type of chili pepper.

Scottadito [Italian]**:** Grilled baby lamb chops.

Seafood chirashi-sushi [Japanese]**:** Sushi rice, assorted vegetables with raw fish on top.

Selle d'agneau aux épinards [French] *(ahNO oh)***:** *Saddle* (loin) of lamb with spinach stuffing.

Seminola pasta: Pasta that is made with durum, a type of wheat that is more coarsely ground than normal wheat flours, used to make pasta, *gnocchi*, puddings, soups, and various confections.

Shallot: A mild-flavored relative of the onion, used for flavoring.

Shanklish [Mediterranean]**:** Mild white cheese topped with onions, tomatoes and olive oil.

Shawarma [Mediterranean]**:** Lamb *marinated* with exotic herbs and spices.

Shepherd's pie [Irish]**:** A dish of cooked ground or diced meat and gravy (sometimes vegetables) topped with mashed potatoes and baked.

Sherry wine: A fortified wine of Spanish origin ranging from pale to dark amber in color and from very dry to sweet in taste, with typically a distinctive nutty flavor.

Shitake [Oriental]: A delicious oriental mushroom used widely in Japanese cookery; now cultivated in the United States, where it is often called golden oak.

Shish kebab: Chunks of *marinated* meat, fish and/or vegetables that are threaded on a *skewer* and grilled or broiled.

Shoofly pie [Pennsylvania Dutch]: A sweet pie with a filling of a mixture of molasses, brown sugar, water and butter – so sweet that one must shoo away the flies!

Shrimp makhni malal [Indian-India]: Jumbo shrimp cooked with mushrooms and coconut in a mildly spicy sauce.

Shrimp tempura roll – sushi [Japanese]: Shrimp tempura (batter-dipped and deep fried), asparagus, *avocado* and made into a *sushi* roll.

Siciliana [Italian]: A pasta sauce made with eggplant and *mozzarella* cheese.

Simmer: To cook food gently in liquid so that tiny bubbles just begin to break the surface.

Sinigaug na baboy [Philippines]: Pork sour soup.

Skewer: A long, thin pointed rod made of metal or wood, often used to hold meat and vegetables in place during cooking, as in *shish kebab*.

Smorgasbord [Swedish]: A buffet meal of various hot and cold foods.

Snapper: The most popular snapper fish is the red snapper, the meat of which is firm-textured and contains very little fat.

Soba noodles [Japanese]**:** A Japanese noodle made from buckwheat flour, which gives it a dark brownish-gray color.

Sofrito [Spanish] (Italian soffrito)**:** A saute of finely-minced garlic, onions, peppers and herbs, used to flavor soups, sauces and meat dishes.

Solomillo [Spanish] *(soloMEyo)***:** Filet mignon (boneless cut of tenderloin beef).

Sopa [Spanish]**:** Hot or cold soup.

Sopaipilla [Mexican]**:** Deep-fried pastry, served with ice cream, honey or flavored syrup. A favorite Southwestern U.S. dessert.

Sorbet [French] (Italian sorbetto)**:** A type of sherbet (also referred to as ices or granitas) which never contains milk, made with a variety of fruits, customarily served either as a palate refresher between courses or as a dessert.

Sorrel: A plant with large spinach-like leaves with a slightly bitter taste, used particularly in sauces to accompany fish and veal.

Soufflé [French] *(sueFLAY)***:** Beaten egg whites with a yolk-based puree and a variety of ingredients, such as cheese, meat, fish, or vegetables baked to rise to a high and light state, and served immediately.

Soup joumou [Haitian]: Pumpkin soup.

Souviaki [Greek]: Chunks of **marinated** meat grilled on a **skewer**.

Soy sauce: A salty, fermented sauce prepared from **soybeans** – common to oriental cookery.

Spaetzle [German]: Potato noodles or dumplings.

Spanakopita [Greek]: A savory pie made of top and bottom phyllo-dough (tissue-thin layers) crusts with a filling of sautéed spinach and onions mixed with **feta** cheese, eggs and seasonings.

Spanakorizo [Greek]: Rice and spinach flavored with mint.

Spring roll [Thai-Thailand]: Appetizer: crisp dough rolls stuffed with vegetables, served with plum sauce; smaller than egg rolls.

Spumone, or Spumoni [Italian]: A frozen, molded dessert: two layers of ice cream between which is a layer of sweetened whipped cream, rum, nuts, and candied fruit.

Stamp and go [Jamaican]: Fried codfish cakes.

Steak au poivre [Madagascar] *(oh PWAV)*: New York sirloin **flambé** with **brandy**, served with green peppercorns.

Steak au poivre [French] *(oh PWAV)*: Steak that is spiced with peppercorns or ground black pepper.

Steak Diane [Swiss]: Butterfly steak *sautéed* with *shallots*, *bordelaise* and cream sauce.

Stock: The strained liquid that is the result of cooking vegetables, meat or fish and other seasoning ingredients in water.

Straccetti [Italian]: Thin slices of protein.

Straw vegetables: Julienne (finely sliced).

Strawberries Romanoff: A dessert of fresh strawberries served on top of vanilla ice cream with strawberry sauce and whipped cream.

Stroganoff [German]: Slices of beef *sautéed* with fresh mushrooms, onions and *burgundy*, blended with a sour cream sauce.

Stromboli [Italian]: Pepperoni, mushroom, sausage, cheese and tomato sauce in a golden pastry dough.

Strudel [Austrian]: A filled pastry usually containing fruit and spices, such as apples, raisins, sugar and cinnamon.

Sturgeon: A north temperate zone fish, known variously for flesh and for caviar.

Sukiyaki [Japanese]: Traditional semi-sweet stew.

Sunomono [Japanese]: Cooked seafood salad.

Sushi [Japanese]: Japanese for "sandwich", sometimes called rolls (maki), usually made with raw fish and other ingredients and rolled in a specially-prepared white rice.

Sushi-nigiri [Japanese]: Thin slices of raw fish seasoned with wasabi (Japanese horseradish) and wrapped around or layered with specially-prepared white rice.

Sweetbread: Organs of a calf, lamb, etc. especially the pancreas and thymus glands, used in a variety of dishes.

Swiss chard: A beet whose large leaves and succulent stalks are often cooked as a vegetable.

Szechwan [Chinese]: A type of traditional cooking featuring dishes that are spicy and peppery with a tendency to be oily, with less seafood.

Szechwan sesame chicken [Chinese]: An appetizer: Cooked, sliced, boneless chicken tossed with a dressing of sesame seed paste, peppercorns, ginger, garlic, vinegar, sugar, and sesame and hot chili oils.

Tabbouleh [Middle Eastern]: Bulghur wheat (wheat kernels that have been steamed, dried and crushed) mixed with chopped tomatoes, onions, parsley, mint, olive oil and lemon juice – served cold, often with crisp bread.

Taco

Taco [Mexican]: A small pancake, or tortilla, rolled round a filling, such as seasoned meat or beans, into a cigar-shape and shallow-fried.

Tagliatelle [Italian]: Pasta in the shape of small ribbons.

Tahini [Middle Eastern] *(tahHEne)*: A puree of sesame seeds blended with olive oil.

Taisho roll [Japanese]: A *sushi* roll made of yellowtail fish, eel, cucumber and a special sauce.

Tamal: Ground meat seasoned usually with chili, rolled in cornmeal dough, wrapped in corn husks, and steamed.

Tamari [Japanese]: Similar to soy sauce (both are made from soybeans) but thicker. Tamari is usually used as a **condiment**, ketchup perhaps being the closest in similarity of use in the U.S.

Tamarind: A tropical tree with a fruit that has an acid pulp used for preserves and made into a cooling laxative drink; the seeds are cooked and ground into meal.

Tandoor oven [Indian-India]: The traditional rounded-top brick and clay oven found in all Indian restaurants, in which a variety of food is baked, identified as tandoori chicken, tandoori beef, etc.

Tapas [Spanish]: Snacks or appetizers, typically served with wine or beer.

Tarragon: A European herb with pungent aromatic leaves used in flavoring pickles and vinegar.

Tart: A small pie or shell of pastry containing jelly, custard or fruit and often having no top crust.

Tartare: Steak tartare is raw, lean, minced beef, often served with a raw egg.

Tasso [Cajun]: A firm, smoky and flavorfully tangy meat that is principally used for seasoning, such as with beans, eggs and pastas.

Tekka [Japanese]: Filet of fresh tuna and seasoned rice rolled in seaweed.

Tempura [Japanese]: Oriental breading, used with shrimp, fish, and vegetables.

Tenderloin: The most tender part of a variety of meats, such as beef, chicken and pork.

Teriyaki [Japanese]: Food such as beef or chicken that has been marinated in a mixture of soy sauce, sake or sherry, sugar, ginger and seasonings before being grilled, broiled or fried.

Terrine: A small deep earthenware dish with a tight-fitting lid.

Terrine de legumes aux herbes

Terrine de legumes aux herbes [French]: Terrine and pâté are in France used to mean the same in reference to pâté – various elegant, well-seasoned ground meat preparations. If cooked in a terrine (a pork-fat-lined container) the pâté is called a terrine. Pâtés may be hot or cold.

Thyme *(time)*: A pungent, aromatic herb used in seasoning.

Tirami Su [Italian]: Italian for "pick me up" – a rich dessert made from coffee-soaked biscuits sweetened with a variety of ingredients.

Tocinillo del cielo [Spanish] *(toeseeNEyo)*: Egg custard.

Toffee: A butterscotch candy of brittle but tender texture made by boiling sugar and butter.

Tofu [Asian]: Bean curd, a pale soft cheese-like substance made from soybean milk, which forms a dietary staple in most east Asian countries.

Tom kha gai [Thai-Thailand]: Creamed chicken soup made with coconut milk and lemon grass.

Tom yum goong [Thai-Thailand]: Thai soup of assorted and spicy lemon grass in a broth.

Tomatillo *(toemuhTEyo)*: A gooseberry relative with lemony taste that resembles a green tomato.

Tonno [Italian]: Tuna.

Tortellini [Italian]: Small rounds of pasta filled with meat and/or cheese.

Tortilla [Mexican] *(torTEyuh)*: A thin, round, unleavened bread prepared from cornmeal or wheat flour, served hot with a variety of fillings and toppings.

Tostada [Mexican]: A crisp-fried tortilla (a very thin pancake of unleavened bread made of corn or flour) topped with various ingredients such as refried beans, shredded chicken or meat, shredded lettuce, dried tomatoes, grated cheese and sour cream.

Tostones [Spanish]: Smashed fried plantain slices.

Tourtiere [Canadian]: Pastry-covered pie containing minced pork or other chopped meat and various chopped vegetables.

Tres leches [Spanish]: A three-milk dessert cake.

Tricolores [French]: Three colors.

Trifle [British]: A dessert of sponge cake spread with jam or jelly, sprinkled with crumbled macaroons, soaked in wine, and served with custard and whipped cream.

Tripe: The lining of beef, pork or sheep stomach, used in a variety of recipes.

Tronchos de pescado [Spanish]: Fish chunks.

Truffle: An underground fungus of the genus Tuber, prized by gastronomes of several millenia for its ineffable perfume and its supposed aphrodisiac qualities – used mainly to flavor cooked foods but sometimes eaten raw.

Truite meunière ou aux amandes [French]: Lightly floured trout *sautéed* in butter and garnished with lemon and parsley or sautéed almonds.

Tuile [French]: The French word for "tile" – a thin crisp biscuit often in the shape of small buckets filled with ice cream and a variety of other dessert ingredients.

Tulipe [French]: A thin cookie that is gathered into a ruffled-flower shape while still warm.

Tumeric: A bright yellow powder used for flavoring and coloring *curries* and other Indian and southeast Asian dishes.

Tuna: A member of the mackeral family, tuna comes in many varieties, the best known being albacore, bluefin, yellowfin and bonito. The flesh is distinctively rich-flavored, moderate to high in fat, firm-textured, flaky and tender.

Tynant: Non-carbonated bottled water.

Udon pasta [Japanese]: Japanese linguini-type (shaped like little tongues) pasta rich in vitamins and minerals.

Vacherin [French]: A dessert consisting of several crisp meringue rings stacked on top of each other on a meringue or pastry base, filled with ice cream, fruits, and a variety of other sweet ingredients.

Veal Oscar [Swiss}: Medallions of veal *sautéed*, served with crabmeat, asparagus tips and sauce béarnaise (a hot and creamy sauce made from butter, egg yolks, vinegar or lemon juice and a variety of different flavorings).

Velouté [French] *(velouTAY)*: A basic white sauce made from veal, chicken or fish stock and a flour and butter blend.

Vermicelli pasta [Italian]: Italian for "little worms" – pasta shaped into very thin strands.

Viand [French]: Meat.

Vichyssoise [French] *(visheeSWAHZ)*: Cold creamy potato soup.

Vidalia onion: A sweet onion.

Vin blanc: White wine.

Vinaigrette: A cold sauce/dressing made from vinegar and oil with seasonings, typically salt, pepper and garlic, most often served with salads.

Vindaloo [Indian-India]**:** A hot, tangy *curry* sauce.

Vitello [Italian]**:** Veal.

Vitello or pollo piccata al marsala [Italian]**:** Veal or chicken pounded thin and fried in butter and marsala wine.

Voivi: Non-carbonated bottled water.

Vongole [Italian]**:** A type of pasta sauce made with clams.

Vorspeisen [German]**:** Appetizers.

Wakame [Japanese]**:** A type of seaweed.

Wasabi [Japanese]**:** The Japanese form of horseradish, of high pungency, eaten raw, freshly grated, with raw fish and sushi (traditional rice rolls), or dried as a powder.

Weisswurst [German]: Veal sausage.

Westphalian ham [German]: A hard ham with a distinctive flavor derived from being smoked over beechwood and juniper.

Whitefish: A member of the salmon family, with high-fat, mild-flavored firm white flesh.

Wienerschnitzel [German]: Milk-fed veal cutlet breaded and *sautéed* in butter.

Won ton (also wonton) [Chinese]: Dumplings stuffed with a variety of ingredients, a staple of won ton soup.

Won ton Soup [Chinese]: Chicken broth with slices of pork, bok choy (Chinese cabbage) and won tons (stuffed noodle dumplings).

Wurstplatte [German]: A platter of sausages and cold cuts.

Yakitori [Japanese]: Chicken skewered with onions and a special sweet sauce, served as an appetizer or entree.

Yakkomein [Chinese]: Noodles in broth.

Yangchow [Chinese]: Fried rice with a wide variety of ingredients added, often eaten as a snack.

Yuca

Yuca [Spanish} *(YOUkuh)*: A root vegetables also called cassava – similar to potato.

Yum woon-sen [Thai-Thailand]: An appetizer of clear noodles, pork and shrimp cooked with mushrooms, lime juice and vegetables, served with a green salad.

Zabaglione [Italian]: A dessert of egg yolks, sugar and wine (typically *marsala*) whisked together over heat until it froths, and generally served in glasses.

Zarzuela [Spanish]: Catalan fish stew.

Zinfandel wine: A dry, red wine with a variety of fruity flavors ranging from lighter to full richness.

Ziti [Italian]: A tubular pasta in short pieces, often baked in a tomato sauce.

Zucchini [Italian] *(zooKEYne)*: Squash.

Zuppa [Italian]: Soup.

Menu Words

$\mathcal{B}$eyond-The-Menu Restaurant Words

Nouvelle cuisine – it's so beautifully arranged you know somebody's fingers have been all over it.
– Julia Child

"It's chicken, lightly battered in flour, dropped on a dirty floor by mistake then sautéed in lemon sauce anyway."

A la carte

Appetite...a universal wolf – Shakespeare

Is there not a sweet wolf within us that demands its food?
– Emily Dickinson

A la carte: A type of ***menu*** on which there is a separate price for each dish.

Alfresco: Open-air dining.

Ambience (also ambiance)**:** Environment, atmosphere (as the interior or exterior of a ***restaurant***).

Antipasto: Italian word for appetizer.

Banquette *(ban-KET)*: A built-in upholstered bench along the wall of a restaurant.

Bill of fare: A ***menu.***

Bistro: A small or unpretentious European wineshop or ***cafe.***

Blue Plate Special: A phrase made popular during World War II (still showing up on menus once in a while as a touch of nostalgia), when inexpensive basic meat-and-potatoes meals were served on large, originally blue plates. There were code words: Adam and Eve on a raft – two poached eggs on toast. Eve with a lid – apple pie.

Bon appétit: French for "good appetite," as those in the U.S. would say "Enjoy your meal."

Bon vivant: A person having cultivated, refined and sociable tastes, especially in the pleasures of the table.

Brasserie (cafe, bistro): A smaller, less expensive *restaurant*, often more exciting, more experimental, less fussy than the more sophisticated counterpart.

Buffet *(buf-A)*: A counter for refreshments. A table set with a varied array of food and drinks.

Cafe: A smaller, less expensive *restaurant*, often more exciting, more experimental, less fussy than the more sophisticated counterpart.

Captain: (sometimes the *Maitre d'* or *Headwaiter*): Supervisor of every step of the table service, including the wine if there is no *Sommelier*. Wears a tuxedo in a formal *restaurant*.

Chef: A skilled cook who manages a kitchen.

Chef's hat (toque blanche): Originally, the pleats of the tall, white chef's hat represented the bars of the ruler's crown. The hat identified the chef as a trusted member of the royal household who would not poison the monarch.

Connoisseur: One who enjoys dining with discrimination and appreciation of subtleties.

Cornucopia: A curved ram's horn overflowing with fruit and ears of grain used as a decorative motif to symbolize abundance.

Cuisine (such as French, Caribbean): A style of cooking. Also the food prepared.

Culinary: Of or related to the kitchen or cooking.

Decor (*restaurant*): The style and layout of interior furnishings.

Degustation

Degustation: The act or an instance of tasting or savoring food.

Diner: A *restaurant* usually resembling a train dining car in shape.

Du jour: *Menu* feature of the day.

Dutch treat: The *restaurant* charge for the group is to be paid not by one person, but by each diner paying her or his own bill.

Enology (also oenology)**:** The science of wine and wine-making.

Entree: The principal dish of the meal in the United States. In France, an entree is more or less an appetizer.

Entremets *(ahntrueMAZ)***:** Dishes served in addition to the main course of a meal.

Epicure: One with sensitive and discriminating taste, especially in food and drink.

Escoffier *(escofeYEA)***:** A French *chef* or a writer on cooking.

Fare: A range of food, for example that which is on a *menu*.

Gastronomy: Good eating or its lore. *Culinary* customs or styles.

Gastronome (Epicure, gourmet)**:** One with sensitive and discriminating taste, especially in food and drink.

Glutton, Gluttony: One given habitually to greedy and voracious eating and drinking.

Gourmand: One who is heartily, perhaps excessively, fond of food and drink.

Gourmet *(goreMAY)*: A connoisseur of food and drink. Today commonly used to mean "high quality", as in gourmet food.

Gratuity: Another word for tip.

Grazing: To graze is to experiment with a menu and/or the experience of dining. Order appetizers only, for instance, or even have drinks at a particularly pleasant bar (or bars, as a pub crawler), then on to another place for an **entree** and/or appetizers (perhaps a Spanish **restaurant** that specializes in **tapas** – Spanish appetizers), and finally to a place that you know makes its own desserts, for cake or pie and coffee.

Gustatory, Gustation: Referring to, associated with, or being the sense of taste, which is composed of the four basic taste qualities: sweet, sour, salty, bitter.

Haute *(HOTE)* **Cuisine:** Artful or elaborate **cuisine**.

Lucullan *(louKULun)*: Lavish, luxurious – as in a Lucullan feast.

Maitre d' – Maitre d' Hotel: Headwaiter, who is usually the hostess or host, in charge of the whole dining room, who may seat customers and make wine recommendations. Wears a tuxedo in a formal restaurant.

Majordomo (Maitre d', Captain)**:** The person who is in charge of the whole dining room.

Menu: The word menu (first recorded in English in 1837) goes back to the French **menu de repas** – the listed items of a meal, later shortened to the single word menu.

Menu degustation

Menu degustation: A sampling of a number of small portions of chef's specialties, all of which he or she has especially chosen. Each order is often for two or more diners.

New World Cuisine: Flavors of South and Central America and the Caribbean, with a touch of Asia.

If the map of the world were a tablecloth and I could choose any place at that table, I would sit at the southern tip of Florida, at the nexus of North America and the Caribbean. My plate would touch Cuba, the Florida Keys, the Yucatan, the West Indies, the Bahamas, and South America.

And if time could tell, I would listen to the tales of voyagers, discoverers, traders and mystics who, in searching for 'The Indies', The Great Kahn, and the riches of China, discovered something much more valuable and enduring: a world of culinary treasures.

Almost instantly, the cuisines of the Old World began to merge with foods of this New World. This evolutionary and inexorable fusion lies at the heart of New World Cuisine.

– Norman Van Aken
Norman's Restaurant
Coral Gables (Miami), Florida

Nouvelle Cuisine: French term for lighter food served in smaller portions, usually with a highly decorative presentation.

Organic: Relating to, produced with, or based on the use of fertilizers of plant or animal origin without employment of chemically formulated fertilizers or pesticides.

Palate: The seat of the sense of taste.

Prix de diner – Prix de dejeuner *(prededeNUR, dejourNA)***:** All meals on the menu are served for one uniform charge.

Prix fixe *(PRES-FEX)*: A complete meal offered at a preset price.

Piquant: Agreeably stimulating to the *palate*.

Pungent: Sharp and stimulating flavor.

Restaurant: The first use of "restaurant" dates back to the 1700s – a Parisian named Boulanger put up a sign in front of his establishment referring to "restorative" soups. From that eventually evolved the word *restaurant*.

Savor (also Savour – British)**:** Taste or smell with pleasure. Savory – that which is worthy of tasting with pleasure.

Smorgasbord (Swedish)**:** A *buffet* offering a variety of foods and drinks.

Sommelier *(sahmulYEA)*: A *restaurant steward* in charge of wines and their service.

Sous *(SUE)* **chef:** An assistant *chef*.

Spa *cuisine*: Light, healthy food, such as broths, salads, vegetables, fresh fruits – the sort a health resort or spa would serve.

Steward: The restaurant manager.

Surcharge: Restaurants use the word surcharge to refer to a service charge (tip) added to the cost of the food – averaging 15 percent of the final bill.

Table d' Hote menu: Table of the host. A type of *menu* that offers various choices among different courses. The price of the whole meal is the price of the chosen *entree* (the principal dish of the meal in the United States).

Tangy: A sharp, distinctive often lingering flavor.

Tapas: Spanish for appetizers.

Taste Buds: An end organ mediating the sensation of taste and lying chiefly on the surface of the tongue.

Tastevin: Silver cup worn around the neck of the *captain, maitre d', majordomo, steward* in a more elegant *restaurant* to show that he or she is also the wine steward *(sommelier)*.

Trattoria: Italian word for cafe.

Vegan *(VA-jun)***:** An extreme vegetarian who consumes no animal food or dairy products.

Good Restaurant Dining: The Ways

Diners ponder, stutter, variously flaunting their ignorance or their pretensions to knowledge.
— M.F.K. Fisher

A wise man always eats well.
— Chinese proverb

You are where you eat.
  – Pamela Fiore

Finding a good restaurant

The critical question: How do you find your way
to the best restaurant? For that matter, what is meant by
the word "best?" The originality and style of the menu
selections; good service; an ambitious wine list; charming ambiance – it all sounds important! To direct us,
there are tried and true recommenders: our friends, and
food critics. Good luck with taking a relative or friend's
word; it helps to know their tastes and preferences.

Another level of criticism is a guide like the Zagat
Survey, which is conducted through referrals not from
professional critics, but diners themselves, who have
sent in their restaurant evaluations on a Zagat form.
See ZAGAT SURVEY on page 130). Of the international
cities for which there is a Zagat Survey, if one of them
is your home, or one which you travel to frequently or
plan to visit, you can send for the latest Zagat, or
request a survey form, fill it out for the city of your
choice, and mail it in, and you will receive a free copy
of the next year's Zagat for that city. According to Tim
Zagat, "If you ask large numbers of people for their
shared experiences, at least on things like restaurants
and hotels and cars and the things they're familiar with,
you're likely to get a better answer than if you ask one
expert who is very often biased one way or another."

Nevertheless, on to the professional critics, bless
them! What would we do without them? Do you
know personally a food or wine critic? Have you ever
accompanied a critic to a restaurant, and watched an
expert at work? The chances are not – there aren't
many critics, and they go to great lengths to remain
anonymous (a wig, an alias...). What makes a good
critic? How does one become a critic?

For those who would like to pursue these questions
in more depth, there is an excellent book, *Dining Out:*

Secrets from America's Leading Critics, Chefs and Restaurateurs, published in 1998 by Andrew Dornenburg and Karen Page, James Beard-award-winning authors of several other food world books. On the front cover is a photo of Ruth Reichl, long-time food critic of *The New York Times,* her face hidden by a broad black hat, caught in the act of taste-testing. The book, which on the inside front cover claims to "demystify the critical process," does just that.

What makes a good critic? There is no required license, no list of requirements, but one would expect a broad knowledge of food, a familiarity with how a restaurant operates, both in the dining room and the kitchen. There is homework: research into areas of limited expertise, a call to a restaurant to ask about ingredients of a dish being evaluated. Traveling and eating in some of the best restaurants is ideal training. What is the goal of a critic? Is it to educate the reader? Critic Ruth Reichl says, "Ultimately, I think my goal is to entertain people...The great thing about great food is that it can bring people real pleasure and enjoyment *every day.*"

Then too, a critic must be an able and stimulating writer. The fact and opinion of the search for quality in all dimensions of the restaurant experience must be expressed with both authority and charm – after all, the subject is one of the major delights of all – dining out. It isn't surprising that Reichl focuses on entertainment.

This pleasure principle sometimes leads critics to make comments that approach hilarity. An example from what you might call a critic's critic, Frank J. Prial: "One wine writer once likened a champagne to 'a young girl in a long white dress in a summer garden.' Another, more succinct but just as imaginative, pondered a wine for a while and then pronounced: 'It has broad shoulders and very narrow hips.' Still others resort to arcane flummery such as, 'It starts well and has a pleasant finish, but it dies on the middle palate.' One of the more creative wine experts around once sipped a glass, raised his head and said, 'Marigolds.' Then he took another sip and said, 'I was wrong; not marigolds. Dwarf marigolds.' "

Good fun, yes, but one is not always amused or for that matter enlightened by a critic's word play. Norman Van Aken, proprietor of the award-winning Norman's restaurant in Coral Gables (Miami), Florida, says, about some critics' reporting: "They should stop being so f-----ing cute. Despite any valid criticism, their basic premise should be that they care. However, that is not what comes across with many critics these days. It's more the well-turned phrase, the double-entendre. It's being cute."

THE FOOD CRITIC ORDERS DINNER

"I'll have the inevitable quiche Lorraine with an elegantly airy custard filling but a disappointingly soggy pastry, the rather bland and textureless gazpacho, and the slightly-dry-from-overcooking calves' liver lightly garnished with tasteless, oily onions.'

Perhaps after all, the wisest approach to finding the best restaurant is to try to check several references. One can't automatically trust other people's opinions without knowing what they value. We are fortunate today to be able to bring into play alongside our friends' claims, a Zagat, a professional critic or two...

And let's not forget the Internet! Microsoft's
Sidewalk Series of restaurant guides (www.sidewalk.com)
and Conde Nast's Epicurious (www.epicurious.com)
both offer very good (if not always up to date)
mini-reviews by regional critics, and a wealth of
additional information, including a way of feeding in
your own opinions.

Yes, dear fellow diner, we do have a more than
reasonable hope for the best. Finally, when seated at
that searched-out restaurant, keep your senses alert:
some people-watching, an ear to what the waiter
recommends, and an eye to what others are ordering;
perhaps choose what the menu claims to be a signature
dish, to get a good, basic introduction to a new dining
experience. Enjoy!

Plan Ahead

This isn't always possible, and it is fun to sponta-
neously pop into a restaurant with no reservation, even
the best ones! – There is of course the chance of a
no-show. Nevertheless, depending upon your
needs/plans/desires – when it matters – it is comforting
to have things all set ahead of time. First would be a
phone call to check on the restaurant's open days and
set hours, the need for reservations, the menu and
wine list, house specialties, prices, and any number
of considerations that might be on your list, such as
appropriate dress and parking convenience. Best of all
would be to go to the restaurant to see for yourself the
size, decor, atmosphere, ambient lighting and sound,
degree of privacy possible. ... Margaret Visser is right:
"Food is never just something to eat."

Hostess/Host Responsibilities

A host is like a general: calamities often reveal his genius.
– Horace (Roman poet)

The guests are met, the feast is set: may'st hear the merry din!
– Samuel Taylor Coleridge

Depending upon the size and importance of the occasion you are planning for, there is much to think about. Under consideration here is a relatively private party.

You should definitely check out the restaurant ahead of time: overall size, general appearance, atmosphere, degree of privacy, choice of table(s), menu (a *prix fixe*, or one set price for all, is the most convenient), wine list, prices, appropriate dress, parking.

Special requests: A cake, candles (yours or theirs), champagne (definitely ask about it if you are considering bringing your own), name cards, type and/or color of flowers, off-menu dishes, diet and health requirements, in general the sorts of things that you are discussing with your guests.

If possible, it is good to be able to order ahead the food and drink. If that isn't to be, let the restaurant staff know and make the appropriate arrangements.

Will everyone arrive more or less at a set time and be seated, or do you intend to have your guests start out in the bar with wine or cocktails? If the latter, what is the method of payment?

Ah yes – the bill. You pay, or is it to be *Dutch treat*? Of course, you will make this clear from the beginning.

If you wish, you could give the restaurant your credit card when you arrive, making it clear that you plan to sign for the entire bill at the end, in private, away from guests. Some restaurants even have menus with no prices, which you could have for everyone in your party. Arrange this ahead of time, of course.

For your sake, I hope the feast is well set – Good Luck!

Reservations

"Can I have a table near the floor?"
"Certainly, I'll have the waiter saw the legs off."
– Groucho Marx

Live by the diner's pledge: "Honor thy reservation!"
Restaurateurs say that from 15 to 30 percent don't
show up. In the 1958 movie *Indiscreet*, Cary Grant
tells Ingrid Bergman that he has made reservations in
two restaurants – she can take her pick. As it happens,
Bergman has already made plans for their dinner. No
more is said, and two important London restaurants are
out of luck. Indiscreet indeed!

Therefore, a better restaurant may ask those calling
for a reservation to give their credit card number, and
make a charge. Others take down the caller's phone
number, and follow up as they see fit, because the truth
is that those who don't honor reservations create a
serious hardship for dining establishments. Come on,
fellow feasters – we want our beloved restaurants to
succeed! Yes, there are many of them out there, but
take a look – at the same time, some are going belly
up.

Call for a reservation at the latest the morning of
your planned dinner. (Give some thought to your day
of choice – perhaps avoiding the day after a restaurant
is closed; things might not be in full gear. On weekends
and holidays, restaurants are more crowded.) For a
more celebrated place, like Le Cirque in New York,
call several days or more ahead. Start by giving your
name (one name only) and asking with whom you are
speaking. This personal touch may ease your arrival.
With a top-level restaurant, it is good to talk with the
maitre d'. It sets a good tone to say that you are looking
forward to dining at the restaurant – you're a repeat
because it's one of your favorite places, a friend
strongly recommended it, etc. Clearly and
simply state name, day and time, number of people.

If by chance you have a gift certificate, coupon, etc. to present, say so. At this point, have any special requests well in mind: Perhaps you've been to the restaurant before, and want to be seated at your favorite table. There are details you may be concerned about, like credit card acceptance, menu and wine choices and price range, valet parking, smoking, senior citizen or disability issues...Of course it is best to limit the number of special requests. Make a quick summary at the end, to help assure that your concerns are understood and have been noted down.

Be sure to call ahead (by 4 p.m. at the latest) to cancel, or to confirm your reservation, at which time you can mention any change in time of arrival or number of guests. Quickly and clearly outline the special requests you had made earlier.

Show up at the appointed time. Early birds should be seated in the waiting area or in the bar until everyone in the party has arrived; then all go in together.

And now a final word from your favorite restaurant: "Honor thy reservation!"

Arrival at restaurant

You arrive at the time reserved, but cannot be seated immediately. Tsk, tsk. Well, you may be seated in the waiting area, or perhaps go to the bar, to order a cocktail or, if you are clever enough to know what the evening's food and wine choices will be, start in on that wine, and hopefully soon be taken to your table. In any event, patience is needed, especially if arriving at a busy time. Nevertheless, also called for is a complaint to the headwaiter if your reservation is not reasonably well-honored. Phyllis Richman, restaurant critic for *The Washington Post*, says, "If you don't want to be pressured into having a drink, hold your ground. 'I think I'll just wait right here' can be the magic words to get you your table."

If you are taken to an unacceptable table (too noisy an area, in an AC draft, not private enough, etc.) politely refuse to be seated and say that you're willing to wait for another table. Remember that when you call for a reservation, you can request privacy, distance from musicians, or what you will.

Alcoholic Beverages

Water taken in moderation never hurt anybody.
– Mark Twain

The trouble with the world is that everybody in it is three drinks behind.   – Humphrey Bogart

When I was younger, I made a rule never to drink before lunch. It is now my rule never to do so before breakfast.
– Winston Churchill

What contemptible scoundrel stole the cork from my lunch?
– W.C. Fields

Quickly bring me a beaker of wine, so that I may wet my mind and say something clever.   – Aristophanes

A day without wine is like a day without sunshine.
– Anthelme Brillaat-Savarin

Wine is the greatest medicine.
– Old Jewish proverb

Now and then it is a joy to have one's table red with wine and roses.
– Orson Welles

God made only water, but man made wine.
– Victor Hugo

Wines

Read up a bit to discover what you like and its price range; then you can make selections with more confidence (see bibliography: "Alcoholic Beverages"). Experiment. Ask your friends. In a better restaurant, you want to be able to discuss with the *sommelier* (wine steward) the wines the restaurant has to offer. Or, perhaps you are ordering from a waiter who doesn't know much more than you do; in any event, the smoothest way to getting a satisfying glass of wine in your hand is to give the subject some thought before you are seated and ready to sip.

How much wine to order? For one person, most restaurants sell wine by the glass. For two persons, there's the split, or half-bottle. A full bottle of wine should do well minimally for three to six, and two bottles for seven to twelve. Feel free to take home any bottle that you have ordered which is not empty.

Choosing wine to complement food: There is no firm rule here. Experiment with this, and develop your own preferences. White for fish and poultry and red for steak is a general recommendation.

"How 'Pinot' is your Pinot Noir?"

Can you bring your own special bottle of wine to a restaurant? In some states (California, for one), yes. Call ahead, to be sure. With some establishments, if the wine you will bring is not on their list, then it is OK. Expect and ask ahead about a corkage fee – a charge for serving your bottle. If both your wine and the restaurant are of better quality, sometimes the corkage fee will be waived if the wine steward gets an introduction to and a taste of your wine.

Suggestions: Hold the wine glass by the stem, so the wine temperature is not affected by hand heat. Breathing: Red wines benefit from allowing at least a few minutes for the bouquet to develop.

Some words the wine steward might use:

Body: Thinness or thickness of the wine, determined by how the wine flows around the inside of a glass as it is swirled (quickly to slowly).

Bouquet: Aroma or fragrance a wine emits as it is swirled – fruity, spicy, flowery, etc.

Flavor: Wine ranges in flavor from very sweet to very dry.

Vintage: Refers to the year the grape was harvested.

Cool it or not?

Red wine: room temperature
White wine: chilled
Rose, sparkling blush, dessert wines: slightly chilled

Wine names:

Varietal: Wine that has the name of the primary grape used in making the wine – Chardonnay, Pinot noir.

Generic: Wines named for the geographic region where grown – Burgundy, Champagne.

Proprietary: Brand name used for marketing.

Types of wine:
Table wine – unfortified white and red wines that accompany a meal (alcohol content 9.4 to 14 percent).

Sparkling wine – Carbon dioxide is added to make the wine, such as champagne, effervescent (alcohol content 8 to 10 percent).

Fortified wine – Wines that are combined with brandy to increase the alcohol content (17 to 22 percent).

Aromatized wine – Wine that is slightly fortified and flavored with fruit, herbs, spices, such as vermouth. Often combined with other alcoholic beverages as cocktails (alcohol content 15 to 20 percent).

Beers:
Basic reference words:

Lager: Generic term for pale, aged beer, most common beer consumed in the United States.

Ale: Generic term for a heavier beer with a higher alcohol content.

Types of beer:
Pilsner: lager beer with a pale, golden color and a strong hops flavor (alcohol content 4.5 to 5.0 percent).

Munchener: Beer made in Munich, Germany – deep brown color, slightly sweet, with a strong malt flavor.

Malt liquors: Lager beers with alcohol content of 4 to 6 percent.

Light beer: Lager beer especially brewed to reduce the number of calories and carbohydrates.

Bock: A dark beer with more than usual body.

Liquors:
Brandy: Liquor made by the distillation of wine or a fermented fruit mash.

Cognac: A well-known brandy distilled in the region near the city of Cognac, France.

Aquavit: Scandinavian distilled beverage the same as gin but with caraway flavor.

Tequila: Mexican spirit distilled from pulque, the juice of the agave plant.

Cordials: Sweet, colorful drinks which must contain at least 2 percent sugar. The European word for cordials is liqueurs. Examples: drambuie, triple sec, creme de minthe.

Aperitif:

An alcoholic drink taken before a meal as an appetizer.

Mocktail:

A cocktail that is alcohol free, but served in typical cocktail glasses with fruit juices and mixers, garnished to resemble regular alcoholic drinks. A Virgin Mary is a Bloody Mary without alcohol.

> *Here's looking at you, kid!*
> – Humphrey Bogart

Toasts

It is natural and pleasant, when family or friends gather for dinner, to wish each other good digestion, health, a long life with joy. Ulysses drank to the health of Achilles in *The Odyssey*. Down through the ages, from the ancient world to today, echo the clinking glasses. (Two theories: Diane Ackerman, in her delightful book *A Natural History of the Senses*, suggests that we touch glasses to add the sense of hearing to the other already stimulated senses. An early Christian belief was that clinking glasses made a bell-like noise to banish the devil, who is repelled by bells.).

Lovers tucked away in a private restaurant booth clink champagne flutes to their mutual passion. Nearby, in a private hall, celebrants, led by the banquet host, pay tribute to an honored guest. (A host was also known early on as a toastmaster: In Henry Fielding's novel *Tom Jones*, published in 1749, there is reference to a toastmaster, who proposed toasts. All present were given the opportunity to offer a toast – more on that later).

Today, we happily continue the charming diversion, seldom pausing during the sipping that follows to wonder why we call a toast a toast. *The Oxford English Dictionary*, our best source for word origins, starts off with a definition that is significant: "Toast: a piece or slice of bread browned at the fire, *often put in wine, water or other beverages*." The earliest use of the word toast: 1430.

Toast was often spiced and/or enriched, adding both interest and sustenance to the drink. Shakespeare: "Go fetch me a quart of sacke; put a toast in it." *The Merry Wives of Windsor*. (Sacke: an amber-colored wine made in southern Spain, for which the English had a taste, but usually found sacke too dry, adding sugar before taking it to market). One can assume that out of its association with beverages came the use of the word toast to refer to a salutation (from the Latin *salus*, health).

A side note: Our current putdown, "He's toast" is actually a late echo of an early 1800s slang expression: "He's had on toast," "served up on a slice of toast," "We've got him now on toast" – meaning done in, swindled.

Toastwater: In the seventeenth century, water in which toasted bread had been steeped, used as a medicinal beverage for invalids. Suggested as the temperance beverage for drinking the health of the king.

1703: A social note: "Every man shall toast his wife."

Top Toast: In 1711, Jonathan Swift refers to Lord Rochester and his fine daughter, Lady Jane, growing up as a "top toast," that is, a lady named the one celebrants honor with a special toast, often the reigning belle of the season.

A toasting glass (eighteenth century): Used for drinking toasts, often inscribed with the name of a belle, and perhaps a verse in her honor. An example from a glass at the Kit-Kat Club in London: "Jove to Ida did the gods invite, and in immortal toasting passed the night."

1852: The novelist Thackeray: "They toasted past and present heroes and beauties in flagons of college ale."

> *This filthy and unhappy custom of drinking healths...*
> – Saint Augustine

Ah, but not all was wine and roses: With the custom of drinking toasts, too often those present were encouraged to propose a swig in honor of any old excuse of a person, event, public official, reigning monarch...In 1628, the English author William Prynne published a book, *Health's Sicknesse*, which suggested a link between toasting healths to the point of drunkenness and the devil.

In response to too much of a good thing, the city fathers in the Massachusetts colony in 1643 passed a law banning the time-honored ritual of toasting, which could go for hours, leaving the revelers hilarious, drunk, under the table. The law was ignored for the most part, and was finally repealed in 1645.

Somehow, the world toasted on, until, in the United States, Prohibition (1920-1934) put a cork on the scene – or did people drink more than ever, and have more fun doing it? A contrasting pair of toasts of this dry period:

> *Here's to Prohibition – the devil take it!*
> *They've stolen our wine, so now we make it.*

> *See our glorious banner waving,*
> *Hear the bugle call;*
> *Rally comrades to the standard:*
> *Down with alcohol!*
> – American temperance groups

And now, dear rallied comrades under today's lighthearted, "up" banner – a heartfelt toast: Good health, good cheer, and may your restaurant experiences be the better for the possession of this charming book! For your greater toasting enjoyment, here are some toasts historic and new, serious and silly, with blank pages at the end for you to add old favorites, new creations, discoveries. Enjoy!

A word of caution: Toasting can get you in trouble! In 1982, President Ronald Reagan rose at a dinner hosted in his honor by the President of Brazil and proposed a toast "to the people of Bolivia!" President Gerald Ford, toasting Anwar sadat in December, 1975: "To the great people and the government of Israel – Egypt; excuse me!" Keep this admonition in mind as you lift your well-meaning glass!

Shakespearean Toasts

I drink to the general joy of the whole table. – Macbeth

Now good digestion wait on appetite and health on both.
– Macbeth

A health, gentlemen, let it go round. – Henry VIII

Fair thought and happy hours attend on you.
– The Merchant of Venice

The best of happiness, honor and fortunes keep with you.
– Timon of Athens

Toasts of the Famous

One sip of this will bathe the drooping spirits in delight beyond the bliss of dreams. – John Milton

Here's to your good health, and your family's good health, and may you all live long and prosper.
– Washington Irving

God bless us every one!
  – Tiny Tim, Charles Dickens' *The Christmas Carol*

*Here's a sigh to those who love me, And a smile to
those who hate; And whatever sky's above me,
Here's a heart for every fate.*   – Byron

*Let us have wine and women, mirth and laughter –
Sermons and soda water the day after.*   – Byron

*Here's to the maiden of bashful fifteen, here's to the widow of
fifty; here's to the flaunting extravagant queen, here's to the
housewife that's thrifty. Let the toast pass, drink to the lass,
I'll warrant she'll prove an excuse for the glass.*
        – Richard Sheridan, *The School for Scandal*

May you live all the days of your life.
          – Jonathan Swift, *Gulliver's Travels*

To peace and friendship among all people.
          – President Jimmy Carter

To long lives and short wars. – Colonel Potter, M*A*S*H

In the words of Star Trek's Mr. Spock: Live long and prosper!

Here's looking at you, kid.
          – Humphrey Bogart, *Casablanca*

General Toasts

*To goodbyes, may they never be spoken.
To friendships, may they never be broken.*

*To our friends, who keep city life from being what Thoreau
called it: "being lonesome together."*

*Here's to those who love us well. Those who don't can go
to hell!*

*Here's to hell. May the stay there be as much fun as the
way there.*

Here's to our hostess, considerate and sweet. Her wit is endless – but when do we eat?

To the sun that warmed the vineyard, to the juice that turned to wine, to the host that cracked the bottle, and made it yours and mine.

Nothing but the best for our hostess/host. That's why she/he has us as friends.

To our host/hostess, who is living proof that God has a sense of humor.

Eat, drink and be merry, for tomorrow we diet.
                                        – W.G. Beymer

May the road rise to meet you, may the wind be always at your back, the sun shine warm upon your face, the rain fall soft upon your fields, and until we meet again, may God hold you in the palm of his hand.   – Traditional Irish toast

Here's to the land of the shamrock so green, here's to each lad and his darling colleen, here's to the ones we love dearest and most, and may God bless old Ireland, that's an Irishman's toast.

Any port in a storm. Any wine, for that matter.

To grape expectations.

Up to my lips and over my gums – look out guts, here she comes!

Here's champagne to our real friends, and real pain to our sham friends.

Amor, salud, dinero, y tiempo para gustarle.
Love, health, money, and time to enjoy it.
                                        – Old Spanish proverb

Here's to a woman who has so improved her community that she can say, as the great architect Sir Christopher Wren said, "If you seek my monument, look around you."

As Dorothy Parker once said to a friend who had just given birth: "Congratulations! We all knew you had it in you."

To the waiter: We drink to your health, O waiter! And may you be preserved from old age, gout, or sudden death – at least 'till supper's served.

Clink, clink your glasses and drink, why should we trouble borrow? Care not for sorrow, a fig for the morrow, tonight let's be merry and drink!

Here's mud in your eye!

International Toasts

Unless otherwise indicated, the toast is *"To your health."*

Albanian: *Se hetan.*
Arabic: *Fi sihtak.*
Armenian: *Genatzt.*
Australian: *Here's looking up your kilt!*
Belgian: *Op uw gezonheid.*
Brazilian: *Saude viva.*
Chinese: *Yam seng. Bottoms up!*
Czech/Slovak: *Na zdravi.*
Dutch: *Provst.*
Esperanto: *Je zia sano.*
Estonian: *Parimat tulevikuks. Best for your future.*
Ethiopian: *Letanachin.*
Farsi: *Solumati.*
Finnish: *Kippis.*
French: *A votre sante.*
Austrian/German: *Prosit.*
Greek: *Stin ygia sou.*
Gypsy: *May you live until a dead horse kicks you.*

Hawaiian: *Havoli maoli oe. To your happiness.*
Hungarian: *Kedves egeszsegere.*
Indian (India): *Sap ki sehat ke Liye.*
Irish: *Slainte.*
Italian: *Salute.*
Japanese: *Kan pai. Bottoms up!*
Jewish: *L'chayim. To life!*
Polish: *Na zdrowie.*
Portuguese: *A sua suade.*
Russian: *Na zdorovia.*
Scandinavian/Swedish: *Skoal.*
Scottish: *Slainte.*
Spanish: *Salud.*
Swiss: *Prosit.*
Thai: *sawasdi.*
Turkish: *Serefe.*
Ukrainian: *Na zdorovya.*
Yiddish: *Zol zon tzgezhint.*

Stag Toasts

Here's to woman! Would that we could fall into her arms without falling into her hands.

To our wives and sweethearts – may they never meet.

Here's to whiskey, scotch and rye, amber smooth and clear – not as sweet as a woman's lips, but a damn sight more sincere.

Here's to the happiest hours of my married life, spent in another woman's arms – my mother!

Curse Toasts

May all your enemies move in with you. – Yiddish

May your retirement plan be supervised by Jimmy Hoffa
                                                    – Steve Allen

May the devil make a ladder of your backbone while he is picking apples in hell.

A plague on both your houses.
                    – Shakespeare, *Romeo and Juliet*

May his soul be forever tormented by fire, and his bones be dug up by dogs and dragged through the streets of Minneapolis.
                                        – Garrison Keillor

Note: See the Toasts heading in the bibliography for a short list of books on the subject published in the nineties.

Favorite Toasts

Favorite Toasts

Paying

There is room for tension here – be careful: Restaurants are often fairly dark, so you can't read the bill very well, and besides you have had a glass of wine or two, and are not in the mood to be calculating. If it matters to you, be assured that it is not bad form to ask for prices when the restaurant's daily specials are orally presented. Is there a charge for splitting or sharing dishes? Has a surcharge (tip) been added to the bill? Does the state or country you are in have a long-standing or recently added beverage tax you don't know about? The list goes on. There may be items priced on both sides of the check, even printed on several pages. Be aware that the way the bill is laid out varies depending upon the establishment, the state, the country. Just because the bill is a computer printout does not mean that human error has been eliminated. It is estimated that 20 to 25 percent of restaurant bills contain mistakes. When Laura, author Vicki's sister, the math whiz, was growing up, it was her delight to check bills and find errors. Once the final add-up was over five dollars in our favor; she walked out amazed that the restaurant said thank you and goodbye – and never noticed!

Seriously, dear diner – always check the bill for accuracy. Nowadays, at the better places (the ones we love, with the charming ambience, delicious food and fine wines), you very often end up staring at a heart-chilling final amount to come up with. Is the bill correct? If you can't read or understand it, ask the server or maitre d' for assistance. Avoid the usual thing of everyone at the table trying to "clarify" things! Feel free to walk over to a quiet, well-lit hallway and add it up twice.

OK – the bill is accurate. Now, who and how to pay? Hopefully, this is known by all from the beginning. Asking the server to split the check between several payers is not acceptable, unless we're talking about two people, and this has been prearranged. Especially for a pricey bill, ask ahead of time if it is OK to divide the final amount between several credit cards. Those on expense accounts who will be contributing to the bill and have special requests should make them known from the start. If you are able to write a check, remember that the tip must be paid in cash.

In the rare case of a disaster – you've left your wallet at home – ask to speak with the headwaiter or manager to see what can be arranged. Is it possible for you to be billed at your home or office? Maybe, especially if yours is a familiar face. Be assured that something agreeable to both parties will be arranged.

There – you're out the door, the stars are bright overhead, the devil has been given his due, and all is well – congratulations!

Tipping (see tip computing chart on inside back cover)

Perhaps the five-pound note I slipped into his hand was
excessive but, lacking a diamond as big as The Ritz,
I had no adequate means of expressing my gratitude.
— S.J. Perelman

It is said that the word tip is an acronym which dates back to the Elizabeth I period expression "**T**o **I**nsure **P**romptness." Diners tossed coins into pots inscribed with the letters. Today we're still tossing coins around, in response to the degree of promptness, pleasantness, the quality of the food and drink. The word gratuity, another word for tip, comes from the Medieval Latin *gratuitas*, meaning present or gift.

We're pretty much used to (This is excluding the tax): Good and prompt service - 15 percent
> Very good to extraordinary service, and perhaps standard in a better restaurant at which several servers are involved - 18 to 20 percent.

Fair service - 10 to 14 percent
Poor service - anything one feels like leaving.

This is fairly straightforward, but there are things to consider. Restaurant managers say that tips are a server's bread and butter; not only that, but also tips benefit customers by keeping menu prices down, since customers are paying the bulk of a server's salary, allowing restaurants to charge less for the food. In that case, let's be generous.

In many U.S. restaurants, in Mexico, and in most European hotels and dining establishments, a surcharge, usually 15 percent, is added to the bill (Exceptions include Great Britain and Spain, where service charges are not always included on restaurant bills). Also, in most cases in Europe it is customary to leave behind any leftover loose coins, as an additional tip (exceptions include Switzerland, Belgium and Sweden). Be aware that in some European countries you may encounter a VAT (value added tax). Many Asian countries add a 10 percent service charge to restaurant bills, and in countries like Japan and Korea, tipping of any kind is rare. As I travel and dine in different countries, I find it most helpful to ask the hotel's concierge about such things as tipping customs in local restaurants.

You have no doubt noticed that the layout and wording of bills varies. For instance, many diners feel that having the surcharge added on to the bill saves then the trouble of thinking about it – just don't forget to notice if the surcharge is there. You might wonder how to lower the already added-on gratuity amount; for that, see the headwaiter or manager. I've seen one bill that stated: "Suggested 15 percent tip. Please feel free to raise, lower or remove this tip at your discretion." Another bill: "For your convenience, a 15 percent gratuity will be added to your check. This is subject to your discretion and can be increased, decreased or eliminated entirely. Thank you!" As a matter of fact, without this statement, a customer who isn't careful might end up paying double. Then too, when paying with a credit card, there is that blank "tip" line on the receipt, which, again for one who isn't noticing, might seem to indicate that as yet no tip has been paid. Finally, I've seen a clever bill that has "A tip table provided for your convenience," which lists the amounts for 15, 20 and 25 percent of your bill total.

The view from the other side: A number of servers feel that having the surcharge added onto the bill discourages diners from offering a larger tip. How about you? Others say that at least that way they get a tip, adding that it is not unusual to receive a minimal tip or none at all. I hereby resolve to be a more-than-ever generous tipper – how about you? When you stop to think about it, one should not punish the server because the food was below average. Another thing to consider is that the various serving personnel often pool the tips at the end of the day; you're not just paying for that one waiter – another reason to be more generous, especially in a top restaurant. All said and done, the places where we dine (Maurice Chevalier said, "I never eat when I can dine.") deserve our respect and support – let's tip our hat to them!

Health

A gourmet who thinks of calories is like a Tart who looks at her watch.
– James Beard

Be careful about reading health books – you might die of a misprint!
– Mark Twain

Vegetarianism serves as a criterion by which we know that the pursuit of moral perfection on the part of man is genuine and sincere.
– Leo Tolstoy

*When we lose twenty pounds, dear reader, we may have lost
the best twenty pounds we have! We may be losing the pounds
that contain our genius, our humanity, or love and honesty.*
                                            – Woody Allen

*I never worry about diets. The only carrots that interest me
are the number you get in a diamond.*
                                            – Mae West

Now good digestion wait on appetite, and health on both!
                                            – William Shakespeare

Let food be your medicine.
                                            – Hippocrates

Let's face it – you are either on or just came off
a diet, or at least have thought about becoming a
vegetarian, exercising more, avoiding this or
that...whatever. Good luck with following health issues
in the press. Honey is indigestible. Men who smoke
may be avoiding prostate cancer. Eating too much
green stuff can lead to an excess of vitamin K, which
helps form blood clots and may lead to a heart attack.
Seriously, I read that somewhere; it must be true!

While we are on America's favorite subject –
health, let it be known that food eaten away from
home in this country accounts for one third of
consumption (Hey, it's a published statistic, so it must
be right, right?) On average, restaurant food has twice
as many calories as the food prepared at home,
especially with some effort to control the big **C.**
Restaurants know that butter and mayo etc. make the
dishes more appealing – fat tastes good! Considering
this and other health considerations, here are some
recommendations for us restaurant-goers.

If you're on a diet, be discreet about it. Don't make
the other diners feel like gluttons as you describe your
food-control program. Guests, notify your host ahead of
time if you must follow doctor's orders, or even that
you must bring your own food.

If you know that you're going out to a restaurant for dinner that day, make breakfast and lunch more moderate-sized.

Eat smart – take your time when eating. The slower you eat, the less you eat (maybe). Enjoy your food. Taste the flavors.

Some restaurants offer half (sometimes listed as appetizer-size) portions. Ask.

You don't have to order an entree. Try several appetizers, salad, soup.

Forget the old adage "Clean your plate." Not applicable in today's more or less "Less is more" world.

Restaurant portions are large – remember that when placing your order. Take-home bags are no longer for dogs only! Eat half, take half home – please!

Eat salad as a first course (dressing on the side, of course). Then hopefully you are a bit sated and can thereafter eat more moderately.

A good old golden rule: Anything in moderation.

This just in: One or two alcoholic drinks a day can shave your risk of heart disease by 30 to 50 percent, regardless of your diet or smoking habits! Red wine retards blood clot formation. Alcohol heightens beneficial HDL levels that cleanse blood vessels of cholesterol. The preventive mechanism found in alcohol can also be found in red grape juice, or just in eating red grapes. Please don't think I'm making this up – I read it somewhere!

Eat fish and chicken baked or broiled, no skin, no oil, and vegetables steamed or microwaved, and not overcooked – you knew this, yes?

Starting on May 2, 1997, a U.S. Food and Drug Administration ruling requires all restaurants to be able to support health or nutritional claims made on their menus. The claim backup does not have to appear on the menu, but must be provided on request. For example, for a "heart healthy" claim, a restaurant has to be able to show the levels of fat, saturated fat, cholesterol, and sodium. Consumers must be aware of portion references: a one-cup health content reference must be extended if the portion you end up with amounts to three cups.

American Dietetic Association Consumer Nutrition Hotline: 1-800-366-1655.

For a complete list of vitamins and what they do, call 1-800-987-7465, and ask for document #202. $4.95.

Visit your local library and book store – the stack of health-related books is mountain-high, and growing. Happy climbing, I mean reading!

"Everything that was bad for you is now good for you."

Smoking

Restaurants today have for the most part arranged smoking and nonsmoking areas as best they can. When making your reservation, specify which you prefer. Even in a smoking section it is not acceptable to light up until after the dessert course.

Complaints/Compliments

This stuff tastes awful; I could have made a fortune selling it to my local health-food store.
– Woody Allen

...seeking the food he eats, pleased with what he gets.
– William Shakespeare

He who flatters the cook never goes hungry.
– Old proverb

A good restaurant should welcome both complaints and compliments – as with most things, it's a matter of style. If your waiter graced your table with good service, feel free to increase the tip, but why not also thank him with a few kind words. On the other hand, bad service should also be reflected in the tip, but feel free to let the server (or perhaps the headwaiter) know WHY you have limited the tip. If you don't do so, the waiter will probably think no further than that you're just another ungenerous, unappreciative patron.

The key here is that the restaurant staff should be really attentive to thoughtfully expressed indications from you that something has gone particularly well, especially to the specific point that you will definitely be back for another such delightful experience, or that the next time you visit the restaurant, you hope that a certain thing or things will be improved. Later, if you are so motivated, write a letter; again, give it the tone that you would expect to be well-received. I once wrote such a letter (calling ahead to get the owner's name and the address), and received a note of appreciation and an offer of a complimentary bottle of wine at my next visit.

Doggie-bag? Yes and No!

No, usually, with a better, more formal, establishment where you're having dinner. Of course, we all do it in average situations – feel free! We know that some restaurants (too many of them, as a matter of fact) really pile it on, and our best diet defense is to take half of it home, certainly not always for the dog! It does seem to be carrying fine manners too far to waste perfectly good food. I have a friend who has a small food cabinet on the rear seat of her car for just that purpose – I've wondered if she sometimes forgets what's back there! At the end of your dinner party, there could be a half-full bottle of wine – it is perfectly acceptable to take it out with you.

"Sorry folks – it's not what you ordered, but everyone is getting fettucine until we fix the computer."

ZAGATSURVEY®
The Perfect Gift

America's Best Meal Deals
America's Top Restaurants
Atlanta
Boston
Chicago
Conn/So. NY State
Dallas/Fort Worth
Hawaii
Houston
Kansas City
Las Vegas
London
London Restaurant Map
Long Island
Los Angeles
LA Marketplace
Miami/So. Florida
Michigan
Minneapolis/St. Paul
New Jersey

New Orleans
New York City
NYC Marketplace
NYC Restaurant Disc
NYC Restaurant Map
Ohio
Orlando/Central Florida
Paris
Philadelphia
Rocky Mountain (CO/UT)
San Diego
San Francisco
Seattle/Portland
Southwest (AZ/NM)
St. Louis
Toronto
Vancouver
Washington, D.C./Baltimore
Also:
U.S. Hotels, Resorts & Spas

TO ORDER:
Call toll free 800-333-3421,
E-mail to zagat@zagatsurvey.com or
visit our website at www.zagat.com

or write to: ZAGATSURVEY®
4 Columbus Circle, New York, New York 10019

$\mathcal{B}$ibliography

Next to eating good dinners, a healthy man with a benevolent turn of mind must like, I think, to read about them.
— William Makepiece Thakeray

Manhattan is a narrow island off the coast of New Jersey devoted to the pursuit of lunch.
— Raymond Sokolov

Grub first, then ethics.
— Bertolt Brecht

A revolution is not the same as a dinner party.
— Mao Tse-Tung

Your local library and bookstore have a very large and growing section on restaurants, food, beverages, health – whatever you're seeking. The printed matter, internet information, audio-video material etc. is so extensive that it is best to get some specific direction from a librarian or store clerk before beginning your search. This list will get you started.

First, a quick comment on a couple of food magazines, of which there are many, most of which are directed toward the at-home cook; you probably have a favorite or two. *Culinary Trends* (printed quarterly), is one that says it was "created by a chef for chefs and the culinary industry," and therefore is more for the international restaurant world. Another one that is along the same lines is *Saveur*. Take a look.

Alcoholic Beverages

Beazley, Mitchell, *Michael Broadstreet's Pocket Guide to Winetasting.* London: Reed Consumer Books Limited, 1997.

Tanzer, Stephen, *Food and Wine Magazine's Official Wine Guide.* New York: American Express Publishing Corp., 1999.

Bradney, Gail, *Best Wines.* New York: The Print Project, 1999.

Clarke, Oz, *Oz Clarke's Pocket Wine Guide.* London: Webster's International Publishers, 1999.

Johnson, Hugh, *Hugh Johnson's Modern Encyclopedia of Wine*, 4th Edition. New York: Simon and Schuster, 1998. The serious wine lover need look no further than Hugh Johnson's encyclopedia for a comprehensive, authoritative and easy-to-use source on the world's wine and winemakers.

Rosengarten, David and Joshua Wesson, *Red Wine with Fish: The New Art of Matching Wine with Food.* New York: Simon and Schuster, 1989. In their introduction, the authors say that "There are no experts on matching food and wine." They go on to sound like experts in several hundred pages of good information about wine and food, with chapters like, "The Gastronomic Hall of Fame: The Ten Greatest Matches We've Ever Known." For both the novice and the aficionado this book is charming and worth reading. In their wisdom the authors' last word is: It's up to you!

Conrad, Barnaby, *The Martini: An Illustrated History of the American Classic.* San Francisco: Chronicle Books, 1995. Even if you don't drink you'll at least try a martini after enjoying this delightful array of martini-inspired art, cartoons, collectibles, advertisements, and film strips. H.L. Mencken called the martini "the only American invention as perfect as a sonnet." Author Conrad and Chronicle Books have indeed produced a handsome, delightful, visually delicious tribute to the martini.

Jackson, Michael, *Michael Jackson's Beer Companion.* Philadelphia: Running Press, 1993. A coffee-table size well-illustrated book on the world's great beer styles, gastronomy and traditions.

General Reference

Dornenburg, Andrew and Karen Page, *Dining Out: Secrets from America's Leading Critics, Chefs and Restaurateurs.* New York: John Wiley and Sons, Inc., 1998. An excellent reference book for the serious reader of food world lore.

Ayto, John, *The Diner's Dictionary: Food and Drink from A to Z.* New York: Oxford University Press, 1993. For those who want to have at home a more extensive food dictionary, this is a lively and authoritative one, with the meaning, origin and development of over 1,200 food and drink terms.

Herbst, Sharon Tyler, *Food Lover's Companion.* Hauppauge, New York: Barron's Educational Series, Inc., 1990. Another A to Z dictionary that gives comprehensive definitions of over 3,000 food, wine and culinary terms.

Ettlinger, Steve, with Melanie Falick, *The Restaurant Lover's Companion: A Handbook for Deciphering the Mysteries of Ethnic Menus.* New York: Addison-Wesley Publishing Company, 1995. The authors say in their introduction that this book is "meant to play the role of an erudite and well-traveled friend who dines with you and explains the meal as it progresses." The book is divided alphabetically into chapters for each country, with background information, menu ordering and cooking methods, and a wealth of additional material. Highly recommended.

Rommelmann, Nancy, *Everything You Pretend to Know About Food and are Afraid Someone Will Ask.* New York: Penguin Books, 1998. A series of basic food questions with short, clear, lively answers. See Chapter 14 – "Dining Out" for a short list of terms typically found on menus of the most popular U.S. and international restaurants.

Vorhees, Don, *Why Does Popcorn Pop?* New York: Carol Publishing Group, 1995. 201 interesting facts about food. There is a short chapter on restaurants, with a focus on fast food. Who was Colonel Sanders? Is McDonald's food the same the world around?

Jacobson, Michael and Sarah Fritschner, *Fast-Food Guide*. New York: Workman Publishing, 1991. What's good, what's bad, and how to tell the difference.

The American Institute of Wine and Food. 1550 Bryant Street, 7th Floor, San Francisco, California, 94103. Phone: 415-255-3000. A not-for-profit organization founded in 1981 by Julia Child, Robert Mondavi and other leaders of the world of gastronomy. Its mission is to advance the understanding, appreciation, and quality of food and drink, enhancing the lives of all people. Contact the Institute to find out about conferences, books, educational programs and events. Publications: *The Journal of Gastronomy*, and *The American Wine and Food Newsletter*.

Barnette, Martha, *Ladyfingers and Nun's Tummies: A Lighthearted Look at How Foods Got Their Names*. New York: Random House, 1997. Example: the word coconut, from the Portuguese word coco, meaning goblin, in reference to the three indentations at the bottom of a coconut shell that resemble a spooky little face.

Mariani, John, *America Eats Out*. New York: William Morrow, 1991. An illustrated history of restaurants, taverns, coffee shops, speakeasies and other establishments that have fed and entertained us for 350 years.

Paston-Williams, Sara, *The Art of Dining: A History of Cooking and Eating*. London, England: National Trust Enterprises, Ltd., 1993. A handsome, beautifully illustrated large-size book of the British world of food, from Medieval to Victorian and Edwardian times.

Egerton, March, Editor, *Since Eve Ate Apples*. Portland, Oregon: Tsunami Press, 1994. "All human history attests that happiness for man – the hungry sinner – since Eve ate apples, Much depends upon dinner!" This quote by the English poet Lord Byron is the source of the title of this book of quotations on feasting, fasting and food from the beginning.

Jones, Evan, *A Food Lover's Companion*. New York: Harper and Row, 1979. A pleasing book of good reading – poems, essays, stories, quotes – by great writers, among them Chekhov, Hemingway, Michener, Woody Allen.

M.F.K. Fisher, *The Art of Eating*. New York: Macmillan Publishing Company, 1990. One of the world's finest food writers – the grand dame of gastronomy. An eclectic array of thoughts, memories and recipes.

Digby, Joan and John, *Food for Thought: An Anthology of Writings Inspired by Food*. Hopewell, New Jersey: The Ecco Press, 1987. "The easiest way to enjoy food without gaining weight or fretting over suspicious ingredients is to read about it," say the authors, and present a satisfying array of short selections by writers of many nationalities, divided into such sections as "Food," "Starters and Soups," "The staff of life," and "Desserts".

Messerli, Douglas, Editor, *Eating Through Literature and Art*. Los Angeles: Sun and Moon Press, 1994. Messerli has created a delightfully witty book on the eating habits of writers and artists of the twentieth century – recipes, writings, illustrations – Whether the reader is hungry for food, literature, or art, these pages satisfy both the stomach and the mind.

Healthy Dining

Duyff, Roberta Larson, *The American Dietetic Association's Complete Food and Nutrition Guide*. Chronimed Publishing, 1996.

Cima, James, Edited by Elizabeth Hurst, *How to Eat more and Lose Weight and Never Diet Again*. JCP Publishing, 1997. "Increase (This is not a misprint) calorie intake, exercise more to gain muscle, reduce water and fat weight, lose inches, change your psysique, increase your health and energy beyond your wildest dreams," claims the author.

Doner, Kalia, *Restaurant Lover's Fat Gram Counter*. New York: Berkley Books, 1995. Quick-reference listings for calories, fats, sodium, protein, carbohydrates, cholesterol. Inexpensive takealong paperback.

Kraus, Barbara, *Barbara Kraus Complete Guide to Sodium*. New York: Plume, 1992. A dictionary listing of over 7,000 brand names and basic foods with their sodium counts.

Montignac, Michael, *Dine Out and Lose Weight: The French Way to Culinary Savoir Vivre*. Los Angeles, California: Montignac USA, Inc., 1995. A bestseller in France since 1987, this book claims to have "the answer" to the good healthy diner's life, but is difficult to read, and needs extensive study.

Netzer, Corrine T., *The Complete Book of Food Counts*. New York: Dell Publishing, 1991. Inexpensive pocket size A to Z listing, "complete" meaning calories, protein, carbohydrates, fat, cholesterol, sodium and fiber.

Piscatella, Joseph, *The Fat-Gram Guide to Restaurant Food*. New York: Workman Publishing, 1998. Piscatella is the bestselling author of the *Don't Eat Your Heart Out Cookbook*. In his newest book he offers, in convenient alphabetical order, the fat-grams, calories and percent-age of calories from fat for over 3,500 restaurant dishes. Be sure to read the introduction, especially the section on how to order healthy in ethnic restaurants (Italian, French, Thai, Cajun, etc.). Inexpensive takealong paperback.

Powter, Susan, *Food*. New York: Simon and Schuster, 1995. Powter is the author of the bestseller *Stop the Insanity*. Both books offer lively, good-humored, timely information about food that is based on really enjoying eating, but with a definite emphasis on the healthy, informed approach. Chapter 5, "Eating Out," pictures menus and makes suggestions about how to order in a healthy way without sacrificing pleasure and satisfaction. There is a focus on women's needs. "Eat, breathe, move, change the way you look and feel forever." See the author on TV's *The Susan Powter Show*.

Sheats, Cliff and Maggie Greenwood-Robinson, *Lean Bodies*. New York: Warner Books, Inc., 1995. Good information on eating lean in different ethnic restaurants. For instance: option charts on Oriental, Italian, Mexican, homestyle, entertainment events, and fats food: pp, 110-113.

Dr. Ulene, Art, *The Nutribase Guide to Fat and Fiber in Your Food*. New York: Avery Publishing Group, 1995. Inexpensive, pocket size, with over 30,000 food products – sounds complete! Includes restaurant meals.

Warshaw, Hope, S., *The Restaurant Companion: A Guide to Healthier Eating Out*. Chicago: Surry Books, 1990.

Internet Online Listings – A VERY partial listing (There are thousands!). Happy surfing!

The Online Epicure (Note: This is a book.) Salkind, Neil J. New York: John Wiley and Sons, Inc., 1997. Finding out everything you want to know about cooking and eating on the internet. Visit the online website: www.onlineepicure.com

Microsoft's *Sidewalk Series* – Restaurant guides to nine American cities plus Sidney, Australia, recommended by *Esquire Magazine's* food and travel correspondent John Mariani. www.sidewalk.com

Food authority John Mariani also likes Conde Nast's *Epicurious,* a restaurant guide which draws on the resources of *Gourmet, Bon Appetit* and *Conde Nast Traveler* magazines. www.epicurious.com

City Savvy – Dining guides for travelers to New York, Los Angeles, Chicago, Boston, Miami, Dallas, Washington, D.C., Philadelphia. For those in the travel, hospitality, communications and new media industries. www.cais.net/citysavvy/index.html

The American Dietetic Association website: http://www.eatright.org/

Magellan Press. See Magellan Press' extensive database of 10,000 restaurants (with links to many restaurant home pages and E-mail addresses) in more than 1,000 U.S. cities. www.magellanpress.com/wtle.html

Restaurant Central – the premier restaurant guide on the net: www.cuisinenet.com

The Beverage Tasting Institute, a Chicago-based library of beverage reviews. Valuable current information for wine and beer aficionados: www.tastings.com

Restaurant Surveys

Zagat – Hosmon, Robert and Terry Zarikian, Editors. New York: Zagat Survey LLC Yearly. 4 Columbus Circle, New York, New York, 10019. The *Zagat* is a comprehensive yearly survey of better U.S., Canadian and London restaurants in many major cities. The survey is based on evaluations from diners. Purchase a copy from your local bookstore, or write *Zagat* asking for a survey sheet. If you live in or near or plan to travel to one of the referenced cities, every year you can fill out a form with your comments, mail it in, and receive a free copy surveying the city of your responses. You will find the *Zagat* very much worth the effort. Internet: www.zagat.com (See Zagat Survey, page 130).

Passport to New York Restaurants. Mariani, John F., and Peter D. Metzer. New York: Passport, 1997.

Toasts

Dickson, Paul, *Toasts: Over 1,500 of the Best Toasts, Sentiments, Blessings, and Graces.* New York: Crown Publishers, Inc., 1991.

Evans, William R. and Andrew Frothingham, *Crisp Toasts.* New York: St. Martin's Press, 1992.

Fulmer, Dave, *A Gentlemen's Guide to Toasting.* New York: Oxmoor House, 1990.

Herman, Jeff and Deborah, *Toasts for all Occasions.* Franklin Lakes, New Jersey: Career Press, 1998

Travel

Take a look in your local libraries and bookstores; people are on the move, and they must be making frequent refernce to travel books – the shelves are groaning with them! The general reference travel guides: Michelin, Fodor's National Geographic Traveler, Berlitz, Rick Steves (The popular Public Television personality has his own travel series), Lonely Planet, Passport's and others all cover the food scene quite usefully, as do the small foreign language/English phrasebooks. There is no doubt a book out there that will give you helpful information about dining well whatever your destination. Highly recommended is the Fodor's Citypack Series, an excellent compact with a full map for each city, and a whole chapter entitled "eat". Be aware that in most European countries, a fifteen percent service charge is added to restaurant bills, plus possibly a VAT, a value added tax. Here is a partial, random list of travel books that focus on food and drink – titles only, alphabetical by country.

Great Britain:

Best Pubs and Inns. Over 1,500 pubs, inns and village restaurants in Britain.
The Glasglow Pub Companion. The essential guide to over 200 city pubs.
The Good Beer Guide to Great Britain. The essential guide for the traveler in Britain for over 70 years.
Passport's Guide to Britain's Best Restaurants. Includes Scotland, Wales, the Channel Islands, and Ireland.
The Whisky Trails. Scotland. A traveler's guide to Scotch whisky.

Canada:

Canada. The National Geographic Traveler. See hotels and restaurants, p. 348.
Discover Canada. Berlitz. Guides the reader to the best local hotels and restaurants - p. 340.
Guide to Eastern Canada. Every section of Eastern Canada is covered, each ending with a listing of hotels and restaurants.
Quebec, Off the Beaten Track. A guide to unique spots. See the "Places to Eat" index, p. 163.
Vancouver, The Ultimate Guide. A full chapter on restaurants, including cafes, vegetarian, late night, expresso bars.
Vancouver, Best Places. Starts off with a full chapter on restaurants, with a star rating, and paragraph descriptions of the top 175 restaurants.

Caribbean/Bahamas:

Bahamas Guide (Open Road Publishing). See Chapter 11, "Food and Drink," plus in every city chapter there are restaurant recommendations.
Caribbean Connoisseur. An insider's guide to the islands' best hotels, resorts and inns, with recommended restaurants for each, including brief appraisals.
Frommer's Series. This guide has a separate dining section for each island.

Central America:

The Rough Guide Series. Each country has a few pages on food and drink: Belize, Costa Rica, El Salvador, Guatemala, Honduras, Nicaragua, Panama.

Copenhagen:

Baedeker's. There is an especially good separate listing of restaurants.

France:

Cheap Eats in Paris.
Eating Out in Provence and the Cote d'Azur. A personal guide to over 220 local restaurants.
Food Lover's Guide to Paris.
France: The Hungry Traveler. Food guide and menu translator.
French Hotels and Restaurants. Rough Guide. The book the French take when they travel at home.
Paris Bistros and Wine Bars. A select guide.
Restaurants of Paris. A Borzoi guidebook published by Knopf, a glorious extravaganza of a book, to carry along on trips to Paris for a lifetime.

Germany:

The Beer Drinker's Guide to Munich.
Germany, Austria, Poland. Rick Steves. A food section for each country.
Germany: The Hungry Traveler. Food guide and menu translation.

Indonesia:

Eat Smart in Indonesia. How to decipher the menu, know the market foods, and embark on a tasting adventure (does not name specific restaurants).

Italy:

Eating Out in Italy. A personal guide to over 150 restaurants.
The True Insider's Guide to Eating in Italy. A traveler's guide to the hidden gastronomic pleasures of northern Italy.
Italy for the Gourmet Traveler. A large book, covering all of Italy.
Italy: The Hungry Traveler. Food guide and menu translator.
Walking and Eating in Tuscany and Umbria.

Japan:

Eating in Japan. illustrated. A small but very informative book about Japanese food and how it is prepared (does not name specific restaurants).
What's What in Japanese Restaurants. A guide to ordering, eating and enjoying food in Japan (does not name specific restaurants).

Russia:

How to Eat Out in Russia. A dictionary and phrase book for the restaurant. How to understand the menu and make yourself understood.

Spain:

How to Eat Out in Spain. Pocket size.

Turkey:

Eat Smart in Turkey. How to decipher the menu, know the market foods, and embark on a tasting adventure (does not name specific restaurants).

The United States:

America's Best Hotels and Restaurants. Mobil Travel Guide. The four-star and five-star winners.
Chicago's Best Restaurants. Chicago's most comprehensive guide to good eating.
The Eclectic Gourmet Guide to New Orleans. Over 200 restaurants rated and ranked.
Gay Guide to the USA. Fodor's guide. A large book that covers many cities, with maps and "eats" section for each.
Gourmet Getaways: A Taste of North America's Top Resorts. Beautifully illustrated.
Insider's Guide to California's Wine Country. Includes Napa, Sonoma, Mendocino and lake countries.
Seattle Cheap Eats. 300 terrific bargain eateries.
The Eclectic Gourmet Guide to Washington, D.C. Over 250 restaurants rated and ranked.
Marcellino's Atlanta Restaurant Report.
New York. A Borzoi Book, published by Knopf, a beautiful, visual treat of a guide, with a whole chapter on where to eat.

Two for the Road

Food in Five Languages: An International Restaurant Guide. English, French, German, Italian, Spanish.

The Vegetarian Traveler. Where to stay and eat if you're vegetarian, vegan, environmentally sensitive – worldwide!

Watch Your Manners!

These are etiquette books. Since we all dine out so often, the watchdogs of the right way to do things all consider restaurant propriety.

Claiborne, Craig, *Elements of Etiquette.* New York: Morrow and Company, Inc., 1992. Chapter 5: "The Restaurant Adventure."

Martin, Judith, *Miss Manners: Guide for the Turn of the Millenium.* New York: Simon and Schuster, Inc., a Fireside Book, 1990. See "Restaurant" in index.

Post, Peggy, *Emily Post's Etiquette*, 16th Edition. New York: Harper Collins, 1997. Chapter 14: "Mealtime Manners." Chapter 28: "Tipping." See "Restaurant" in index.

Post, Elizabeth L., *Emily Post's Advice for Every Dining Occasion.* New York: Harper Collins, 1994. Chapter 5: "Restaurant Etiquette: Menus, Manners and Maitre d's."

Un bon repas doit commencer avec la faim.
A good meal ought to begin with hunger.
— French proverb

In the Lord's prayer, the first petition is for daily bread.
No one can worship God or love his neighbor on
an empty stomach. — Woodrow Wilson

BON APPÉTIT!